C0-AZH-780
ALMA, MICHIGAN

Many believe that urban intensification is a fiscally and environmentally responsible alternative to urban sprawl with the potential to make our cities more interesting, liveable places. Urban intensification encourages the efficient use of land through conversions, infill, redevelopment, reuse, and suburban densification, and applies to commercial, industrial and institutional properties, as well as residential uses. Its objectives include higher population densities, more efficient use of infrastructure, a greater mix of uses and greater efficiencies between these uses. Frank Lewinberg put it well when he said compact development means "less pavement, shorter pipes, less maintenance, less distance to travel and shorter journeys to work."

The arguments in favour of urban intensification are simple and straightforward. Closer proximity between destinations means fewer car trips, resulting in a reduction of pollution. The time and energy presently invested in building and upgrading infrastructure could be invested in the places in which we reside. And, development remaining within existing urban envelopes would not encroach on farmland and natural areas.

Implementing urban intensification is far more difficult and complex. Many powerful forces influence urban growth: the expanding global economy; local political expediency; traditional expectations of the development industry; changes in retail practices; consumer demand; taxation; new telecommunication technologies; the mobility of multi-national companies; and the fluctuations in legislation affecting local governments. Urban intensification would require resistance to many of these pressures.

A Practitioner's Guide to Urban Intensification is a selection of articles from *The Intensification Report*, the bimonthly journal produced by the Canadian Urban Institute between 1993 and 1996, established with the support of the Ontario Ministry of Housing. This publication consolidates some of the best thinking of the time on the subject.

A Practitioner's Guide to Urban Intensification discusses a variety of "tools" used to intensify urban areas. Several articles examine the logic of intensification, while others review the obstacles to its implementation. The guide contains a critique of neotraditionalism and an examination of the global, regional and local impacts of new telecommunications technologies.

A Practitioner's Guide to Urban Intensification is a rich source of ideas and encouragement for those who wish to affirm the urban characteristics of our cities and for those who have the will to challenge the established development patterns of the past 40 years.

Janice Emeneau

> The arguments in favour of urban intensification are simple and straightforward ... (but) .... implementing urban intensification is far more difficult and complex.

Table of Contents

Consequences of Continued Sprawl

A Growing Concern
1

Costs
2

Public Mind-Set
4

Urban Sprawl and its Consequences. (abridged) Engin Isin

Vol. No. 1, March-April 1993.

Concerns about the detrimental consequences of sprawl have entered the planning debate in North America, Britain and Australia.

Some Thoughts about Intensification. Frank Lewinberg

Vol. No. 1, March-April 1993.

Low density development at the urban fringe has an effect on mobility, land consumption, and infrastructure. Is the development industry catering to an innate preference for single family dwellings or is an artificial demand created through marketing?

Past, Present, Future: Where are We Headed? John Sewell (originally published as "Greenwood: An Opportunity for a new Planning Approach,") (abridged)

Vol. No. 9, July-August 1994.

Infilling and redevelopment were the norm in cities from time immemorial. Now, society appears convinced that increased open space, single use areas and an absence of public street life constitute good planning.

A Toolbox of Intensification Ideas

Main Streets
5

Neighbourhood Support
8

Urban Design Principles
11

Housing on Toronto's Main Streets.

Andrew Farncombe

Vol. No. 4, September-October 1993.

The Main Streets initiative is about increasing population densities along major arterial roads. This article documents the initial steps of the Main-Streets strategy of the City of Toronto.

Bedford Glen: A Designer's Role in Achieving Intensification. Leslie Coates

Vol. No. 5 November-December 1993.

Bedford Glen is a successful medium density development within a low density neighbourhood, a collaborative effort of the designer, the developer and the surrounding community. Good design was the pivotal factor in shaping positive attitudes towards this intensification project.

Greenwood Racetrack: An Opportunity not to be Missed. Ken Greenberg

Vol. No. 9 July-August 1994.

The challenge in redeveloping a piece of land in the heart of one of Toronto's best loved neighbourhoods is to determine the appropriate scale and complexity. Greenberg recommends some design principles.

Taxation
13

Property Taxation and Urban Sprawl.   Enid Slack

Vol. No. 8 May-June 1994.

When property taxes do not relate to services and benefits, there is an impact on development decisions. This article debates the effectiveness of using taxation to implement higher densities.

Conversions
15

Sprout: An Innovative Starter Home.   Sevag Pogharian

Vol. No. 12 January-February 1995.

Sprout is an innovative starter home, designed so that it can be easily modified as family needs change.

Employment
20

Industrial Lands Strategy: City of Vancouver Draws the Line.
Christina DeMarco

Vol. No. 13 March-April 1995.

Although converting under-utilized industrial areas to residential use is an effective way to intensify, the author contends that some inner city industrial land should remain to provide local employment.

Site
Remediation
23

Quantitative Risk Assessment for Contaminated Sites: A Tool for Intensification.
Scott MacRitchie

Vol. No. 13 March-April 1995.

Quantitative Risk Assessment (QRA) is a method to determine clean-up levels on vacant industrial land. QRA is required in the successful implementation of redevelopment policies on sites with possible contamination.

Infill Housing
26

Greenbelt Alliance on Infill Housing. Greenbelt Alliance

Vol. No. 14 May-June 1995.

Infill housing utilizes existing infrastructure, increases levels of safety through natural interactions in shared spaces, alleviates traffic congestion by reducing commuting, and makes mass transit more viable.

Tackling
Superstore
Sprawl
28

Tackling Superstore Sprawl.   John Weiler

Vol. No. 14 May-June 1995

Superstores cater to our love affair with the car, the demand for cheaper goods and our passion for convenience. The author outlines the problems accompanying large format retailing and the reaction to these problems, in Ontario and world wide.

Pricing Goods
& Services
31

Pathways to Sustainability. (abridged) Igor Vojnovic

Vol. No. 15 July-August 1995.

The author contends that goods and services should be priced in accordance with their replacement value. This would lead to a more compact, efficient form of development and minimize resource depletion.

Shared Ownership
35

Rethinking Ownership. Russell Mawby

Vol. No. 17 November-December 1995.

Home ownership in partnerships offers a desirable alternative to renting and an affordable option for downtown living. It would use existing housing stock and intensify the population levels in downtown neighbourhoods.

Understanding Densities
37

Density and Urban Form: Sorting out the Confusions. John Hitchcock

Vol. No. 12 January-February 1995.

Urban density can be a misleading term. The author explains parcel density, street density, gross residential density, and gross municipal area density.

Density and Quality of Life

A Sense of Place
40

Suburbia on the Edge. Lois E. Nesbitt

Vol No. 7 March-April 1993

As edge cities sprawl over the countryside a sense of "placelessness" has evolved. Rather than following the American tradition of seeking new frontiers when dissatisfied with current arrangements, the author suggests that edge cities should be retrofitted and improved.

Safety
42

Partners in Crime. Lance Naismith

Vol. No. 8 May-June 1994.

A multi-disciplinary approach is the most productive to studying urban issues. The opportunity factor in crime can be reduced through good urban design and the creation of "defensible space".

Equity Issues
46

On Intensification and Women - Friendly Cities. Kim England

Vol. No. 11 November-December 1994

There are significant advantages to compact, mixed use development for working women with children. The segregation of land uses reflects the realities of the 1950s and 1960s, rather than women's roles in society today.

Cars
48

Does Sustainable Transportation mean Cities without Cars? Richard Gilbert

Vol. No. 11 November-December 1994.

Emissions from transportation sources are increasing. This study concluded that while higher densities are desirable in reducing the need for a car and the promotion of transit, the mixing of uses may be an even more important element.

Telecommunications Technologies: The Implications

Global
51

Cities in the Information Age.   Pamela Blais

Vol. No. 11 November-December 1994.

As "back office" functions locate to the suburbs, exurbs or other countries, the demand for office space in downtowns diminishes, yet downtowns require diversity to remain viable. The author argues that each aspect of the city should be understood as it relates to global competitiveness.

Regional
54

The Challenge for Public Transit in the Telecommunications Age.
Frances Frisken

Vol. No. 11 November-December 1994.

Advanced telecommunications technologies have facilitated the decentralization of facilities into the new low density suburbs. This dispersion increases the need for private automobile trips.

Local
56

Telework and its Impact on Urban Form.   Penny Gurstein

Vol. No. 11 November-December 1994.

More and more people are working out of their homes. This phenomenon may enhance the desirability of localized work related services, such as telework centres, cafes, bookstores, and copy shops. The neighbourhood may become valued as sensory relief from the computer screen.

Innovative Development Practices: The New Urbanism

New Development Standards
59

Village of Morrison: Community Building Practices.   Marvin Green

Vol. No. 1, March-April 1993

The article describes a suburban development based on reformed ideas on the environment, transportation, household composition, economics and aesthetics. It includes an integrated mix of housing types, architectural styles and forms of tenure.

Live, Work, Play?
62

Is the Neotraditional "Revolution" Likely to Occur? Frank Clayton

Vol. No. 7 March-April 1994.

Neotraditional planning with its underlying premise of integrating where people live, work and play is unworkable. In the author's opinion, planning should not attempt to aggressively alter human behaviour; urban form should be determined by the marketplace.

Designer Suburbs
65

Designer Suburbs.   Hok-Lin Leung
(formerly published as "Density and Quality of Life")

Vol. No. 12 January-February 1995.

Governments that assume neotraditional communities will provide affordable housing are mistaken. Leung suggests "designer suburbs" are simply the new rage for the elite.

Constraints

**Planning -
Too Weak
67**

Residential Intensification: The Wrong Planning Debate. Ray Simpson

Vol. No. 1, March-April 1993

The public does not share the planner's desire to live in intensified communities and the amount of housing potential from intensification has been vastly overstated. The author also contends that land use planning is too weak a tool to combat the strong economic and social forces opposed to intensification.

**The System
70**

Legal and Financial Constraints Impede Intensification. Ron Kanter

Vol. No. 3, July-August, 1993.

Zoning, development charges, assessment practices and official plans can serve to inhibit intensification efforts. The author details steps that could be taken to remove these constraints and to provide incentives for intensification.

**Building Codes
73**

Main Streets Initiative Handicapped by Building Codes   Eberhard Zeidler
(originally published as *The Single Stair and Housing on Main Streets Blues*)(abridged)

Vol. No. 4, September-October 1993.

Restrictive North American building codes need to be relaxed in order to accommodate European style apartments. He then outlines the advantages of the European prototype.

**Public Support
75**

Sprawl and Intensification.   Ken Whitwell

Vol. No. 17 November-December 1995.

Intensification lacks the support of groups that might be expected to uphold such efforts. These groups include rural communities, environmental groups and those in control of building standards and land use regulation.

**Private Property
Rights
77**

To Whom do Things Belong? The Limits of Intensification. Alan Waterhouse

Vol. No. 17 November-December 1995.

There are tensions between the overall public good and private property rights. Intensification will have to wait until this dichotomy is resolved.

**Policy
Compliance
80**

Suburban Intensification in the GTA.   Ray Tomalty

Vol. No. 17 November-December 1995.

The benefits of intensification are often regional in nature, while the costs are born at the local level. While the province may have the motivation to promote intensification policies, it has limited ability to influence land use planning at the local level.

Consequences of Continued Sprawl

Urban Sprawl and its Consequences

Engin Isin

Engin Isin was the Managing Editor of the Intensification Report and is currently a Professor of Urban Studies at York University

The Canadian Urban Institute, since its founding in 1990, has engaged in research projects to explore innovative initiatives in intensification - developing and redeveloping urban land at higher densities than has been customary. With the support of the Ontario Ministry of Housing, we set up an Intensification Resource. As part of this initiative, we launched The Intensification Report, a bi-monthly newsletter designed to serve as a forum for the debate on intensification issues as well as a source of information on various initiatives.

To many, the concern about intensification may seem rather odd. When you look at a map of Ontario, you immediately notice the huge land mass and the concentration of the population in Southern Ontario. But a closer look reveals something else. The high growth rates are concentrated not in the large cities and towns such as Toronto, Hamilton, Ottawa, Windsor, Sudbury, and Timmins but rather in smaller cities and towns (e.g., Brampton, Oakville, Vaughan, Markham, Gloucester, Kanata, and Aurora). This trend of urban growth in what Statistics Canada calls "urban fringe" municipalities has been remarkable in the last twenty years and has picked up during the most recent five years.

We should not be surprised then that "intensification" should have emerged among city planning and policy professionals in the 1980s in reaction to the detrimental consequences of sprawl: traffic congestion, declining transit ridership, increasing infrastructure costs, environmental deterioration, disappearance of prime agricultural land, declining quality of life in low-density neighbourhoods, and so on.

These concerns about the consequences of sprawl are neither new nor restricted to Canada. Since the 1930s, and particularly in the postwar era, urban sprawl has been a major concern in Europe, North America, and Australia. The "containment" of urban growth - the British phrase for intensification - has been a major planning concern in postwar Britain. "Growth management" - a rough equivalent of Canadian "intensification" - has been a prominent feature of planning in hundreds of American cities and towns. Australians call it "consolidation." There the issue has been the subject of heated debate, culminating in a recent Commonwealth Committee report.

In Ontario, the provincial government has adopted several policies to encourage increased densities in our urban and suburban communities. New instruments have emerged to achieve higher densities: redevelopment, infill, suburban densification, and conversion.

However, neither the negative consequences of sprawl nor the benefits of intensification are universally accepted. Proponents and opponents of sprawl continue to debate these issues. As the debate continues, many communities across Ontario have been experimenting with innovative policies and projects to make better use of existing land and infrastructure without opening up virgin land for low density settlement.

The Intensification Report became a forum for those engaged in housing policy and research or involved in intensification issues.

Some Thoughts About Intensification

Frank Lewinberg

In this paper I focus on intensification at the edges of our cities, in the suburbs and smaller centres. That is where the issues of growth are to be joined politically and practically in the next decade and where there is a wide divergence of opinion as to the way forward.

The word intensification usually implies that there be more development on a site than in the typical suburban model. But the real question is how to develop an urban form that meets the needs of the new environmental consciousness and deals comprehensively with social, economic, and mobility issues. We need to find a word that is more inclusive and one that is differentiated from previous cycles of suburban growth. Sustainable is the best I can offer for now.

It is time to change the way we build suburbs.

We all accept the need for growth. It is desirable. Canada has the need and the capacity to accept many more people over the next few generations. Our cities will and must grow to accommodate this additional population. The question is how to shape this growth.

It is not a matter of taste or market preference. We are learning that our society is consuming too much land in a costly and environmentally inappropriate manner. It is part of our deficit-ridden mentality, that we have pushed off to tomorrow the costs of today's excesses.

A new approach is being reflected in the work of David Crombie and the Sewell Commission in Ontario. This new approach did not start with the NDP government in Ontario nor will it end with it. It is instead a change that is evident across Canada, the USA, and Australia.

We need to use our land more wisely. We once allowed industrial pollution and left future generations with the task of cleaning it up. Until now we have ignored the environmental and economic costs of sprawl.

Mobility

First is the question of mobility, which has made the excesses of the past 40 years possible. We know that if we add a lot more people there will either have to be more and wider roads, or more public transit. In North America we have behaved as if we all have the right to perfect mobility. No matter what the public expense or the environmental consequences, the roads should be built so that we can all go from here to anywhere with ease, without delay and all at the same time, including during peak hours. We can no longer afford this excess. Instead we need to make public transit, supported by walking and cycling, a viable alternative.

Transit-supportive planning is environmentally, economically, and socially sustainable. It means ensuring that we build with sufficient density to provide enough potential passengers so that a public transit system can be run economically and effectively. For transit to work, people need to be able to go between transit and their homes easily, comfortably, and safely. Thus sustainable development will need to be sufficiently dense and designed to accept the reality of transit. It's not difficult; it is being done in Canadian cities and around the world.

Consuming land on the suburban frontier

The manner in which we first make our mark on the natural landscape is hard to change later. It is one of the most

Frank Lewinberg is a Principal with Berridge Lewinberg Greenberg Dark Gabor, Ltd.

The costs of sprawl affect us all and are not publicly acknowledged or counted in encouraging more sprawl. The additional pavement, the spread and maintenance of public and private services to a few homes over a large area, are borne by both home buyers and the public. Ultimately we all pay.

visible signals of society's values. Our generation will be judged by how we deal with this frontier. There is no doubt that we need to save the mature forest, the sensitive marsh, and more land at the river's edge. We have learned that we need to allow the earth to filter rain in order to protect rivers, lakes and wild life. Thus we must leave more land in its natural state.

The fact that there will be more people to make the transit work means that we may need more land for schools, recreation and other community needs. Using land for public purposes is an obvious necessity; unfortunately the amount used has gradually increased while the number of people served has declined. We must learn how to build using less land.

Subsidizing the suburbs

The costs of sprawl affect us all but are not publicly acknowledged or accounted for in our development practices. The additional pavement, the length of utilities, and the spread and maintenance of public and private services to a few homes over a large area are all borne by both home buyers and the public. Ultimately we all pay. There is emerging research in the USA and Australia that is beginning to put hard numbers to the social costs of sprawl.

Compact development means less pavement, shorter pipes, less maintenance, less distance to travel, and shorter journeys to work. The Regional Municipality of Ottawa-Carleton estimates a direct private cost saving of up to $9,000 per housing unit through relatively modest intensification. No one has yet estimated the public saving. It is time to remove these excesses, which add to public debt and ultimately make the home less affordable.

What about the developers?

It makes no difference if market surveys show that people prefer lower density single family homes on 60-foot lots. People record their preferences by

buying and renting what is produced. They can take only what is offered and what they can afford. What is offered depends on our developers and our regulators.

We have decided as a society that we no can no longer afford choice in allowing industries to pollute the lands and the rivers. It seems to me we no longer have a choice in the way our cities grow. If the only product available was a sustainable form of housing, work place, and shopping, then there would be no alternatives coming onto the market.

The Canadian development, design, and building industry is very resourceful and highly skilled. It will soon invent a range of products that will not only satisfy but excite the buyer and the renter into a sustainable and likely a more intense form of suburban living.

Every business person knows that if you sell more homes there will be more money to be made. Thus as developers are forced to give up more land for parks, schools, and environmentally sensitive lands, the number of homes and other things they can build at low density falls. However, if they were permitted or even required to build more houses on the land left to them for development they would surely still make money.

If the new rules apply evenly, all the new product will be produced under the same rules. Then it is up to innovation, ingenuity, marketing, and other means to differentiate between products, as it is at present and always has been. Developers are mostly interested in certainty. They want to know that they will be permitted to build, that the sewers and other services will be there, and that rules will not change in mid-stream. Developers want clear as-of-right rule that apply equally.

The future

The physical form of the suburbs must change, but that does not mean that the suburbs will be totally different. Large sections already exist and will remain intact, and the future will still be dominated by home ownership for families.

It makes no difference if market surveys show that people prefer lower density single family homes on 60-foot lots. People record their preferences by buying and renting what is produced. They can take only what is offered and what they can afford.

The existing low density suburban neighbourhoods built between the 1950s and the 1980s will not go away. Instead, they will become more valuable as their supply becomes finite. Even neighbourhoods built only 10 years ago will become the nostalgic, expensive, and desirable older neighbourhoods of the suburbs. As time goes by they will be seen like the older neighbourhoods of cities like Toronto, an historical resource that should be maintained, stable and untouchable.

The new neighbourhoods will also be pleasant. There are already sufficient examples around to illustrate that they do not have to be high rise, that they will still include a large component of single detached and attached freehold homes on their own plot of land. Apartments in medium-rise buildings of 5 to 10 storeys fit in well in this context. Mixing the land uses could make the communities more interesting and more efficient.

The future can be quite attractive, some think even better than the past. I do.

Past, Present, Future: Where Are We Headed?

John Sewell

Intensification is best seen as a code word: it represents a development style which hasn't been pursued in North America for half a century.

Infilling and redevelopment was the norm in city building from time immemorial. Not until the rise of the modern movement at the end of the nineteenth century, and then the implementation of its ideas in between this century's wars and depressions, has intensification ever been thought unusual or undesirable. Modernism enticed most of us to believe that increased open space, single use areas, and an absence of public street life, were the best values to follow in building a city.

And so from the end of the Second World War, particularly in North America, cities have re-adjusted their planning regimes to encourage sprawl and city-thinning, and prevent intensification and infill. As we know, city densities have fallen precipitously and some cities (Detroit is a prime example) have collapsed like dead stars into black holes.

While the problems created by the modern planning vision are becoming more and more evident, the financial ramifications are most worrisome, as modern cities find they can only work with massive subsidies for transit and housing, and those subsidies are drying up - a cultural lag is apparent. Most ordinary people have yet to question their allegiance to modern planning ideas. They continue to believe in the values of open space, single use areas, and an absence of public street life as the basis for good planning.

Communities asked to consider change often say they want more parks - the quintessential modern solution to city building. Many people believe that an intensity of building and street life might be just what is needed for holidays (whether New York or Paris), but they believe it is not acceptable for everyday life.

John Sewell was formerly Mayor of Toronto as well as Chair of the Commission on Planning and Development Reform in Ontario. He is also a journalist, lecturer and community organizer.

A Toolbox of Intensification Ideas

Housing on Toronto's Main Streets

Andrew Farncombe

Andrew Farncombe wrote this article in the fall of 1993 as a graduate student in the faculty of Environmental Studies at York University. He is currently Project Manager for the International Programs Office of the Canadian Urban Institute.

Editor's Note: The final criteria for the design of the City of Toronto's Main Streets initiative are contained in By-law 1994-0178 and were incorporated into the new City Plan, after approval by the Ontario Municipal Board, in 1995.

Toronto's Main Streets initiative is about encouraging modest residential intensification along its network of arterial streets. It is not a new brand of urban planning, but rather an approach which aims to reinforce an existing and successful development pattern - housing above shops along commercial strips. This has been an important part of Toronto's urban fabric since the 19th century.

Proponents of main streets intensification submit that the initiative has several benefits. They claim it will: 1) add to the City's stock of housing (especially affordable units); 2) favour small-scale developers and landowners; 3) support a mixture of commercial and residential land uses; 4) add vitality to the public realm; 5) improve the physical appearance of these arterials; 6) use soft and hard services (especially transit) more efficiently; and, 7) reduce car dependence.

The Main Streets concept can be viewed as being both environmental and entrepreneurial — environmental because it promotes compact urban form, and entrepreneurial because it facilitates development of small sites by individual landowners.

The sorts of redevelopment envisioned under the initiative include infill on vacant lots, redevelopment of under-utilized sites such as plaza-type developments, adaptive re-use of buildings not originally intended for residential uses, and conversions and additions to existing buildings.

The program's principal objective is to create a regulatory environment that provides enough incentives to stimulate incremental housing production yet with adequate controls to discourage land assembly and massive redevelopment. Whether Main Streets can achieve this formidable balancing act will be the initiative's ultimate test.

Initial Proposals

The original vision for Housing on Main Streets was set forth in 1987 by Richard Gilbert, then a municipal politician, at a time when Toronto was experiencing a serious shortage of affordable housing. Gilbert viewed Main Streets intensification as a unique opportunity to create much needed housing without disturbing the city's established neighbourhoods. His report inspired City Council to request the preparation of a feasibility study for main street redevelopment.

The results of the feasibility study were published in the October 1988 *Housing on Toronto's Main Streets Proposals Report*, by the Planning and Development Department. It undertook a preliminary analysis of the constraints and opportunities to Main Streets intensification and presented a comprehensive strategy which the City was to follow in formulating the policy. With Council approval and with funding commitments in place from both the Province and Metro Toronto, Main Streets was officially launched.

Information Collection and Analysis

In the wake of the proposals report came several information-oriented activities which laid the groundwork for Main Streets policy formulation. Activities included:

- Search for Ideas Competition — In 1990 the City sponsored an international architectural competition to generate innovative and workable approaches to housing design in the main streets context.
- Parking Study — A consultant's study surveyed automobile ownership

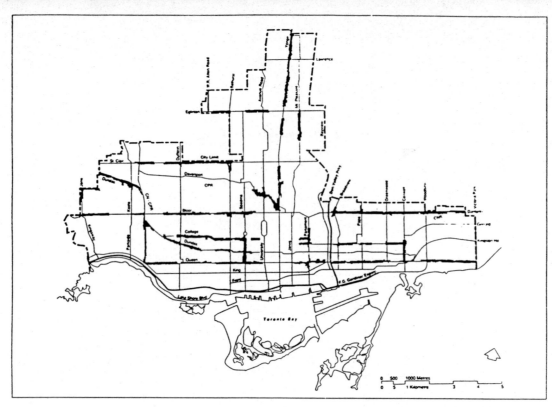

Toronto's main streets are more than commercial centres for the neighbourhoods through which they pass - they are a framework that holds the city together. The darkened segments represent areas in which the potential for more housing has been studied.

patterns of current main streets residents, and recommended a substantial reduction in parking standards.

• Economic Feasibility Study — Planning and design consultants examined the economic feasibility of housing production on Toronto's main streets. The study suggested that reduced parking standards, a five-storey building envelope and a streamlined zoning system would result in the production of 15,000 to 35,000 new units.

• Community Outreach — Planning staff undertook a public participation program which aimed to inform and receive feedback from the community on the program.

• Building on Main Streets Study — A third consulting firm synthesized the information and ideas generated from the design competition and recommended a method for determining an appropriate regulatory framework for Main Streets.

Implementation Strategy

In July 1991, the City released "Principles and Proposed Strategy for Implementing the Main Streets Initiative." It advocated a 'base case envelope' and 'modifier' approach to amending the Official Plan and Zoning By-law. This approach recognized the problems associated with adopting standardized zoning provisions city-wide, given the unique characteristics and context of each main street segment. Instead, zoning designations would be contextualized using a street-by-street, block-by-block analysis. This would produce "tailor-made as- of-right zoning".

The 'base case envelope' set some elementary rules for main streets. It established a five-storey height limit, a 25-metre maximum lot frontage, a rear setback using a 45-degree angular plane to protect adjacent residential properties, a density of three times lot coverage, reduced parking standards, and a formula for determining the shares of permitted land uses.

The 'modifiers' were criteria to be used to adjust the 'base case envelope' either upwards or downwards according to local context. For instance, heights could be adjusted to correspond to street width, higher buildings could be permitted at landmark corner sites and near subway stations, heights and setbacks could be altered to be more sensitive to existing historic buildings and other abutting land uses, and so on. Furthermore, the strategy gave priority to and provided certain incentives for the development of small sites.

All this was to be implemented in three phases. The first, and perhaps the most critical phase, was to apply the proposals to four demonstration areas. These were to test and fine-tune the proposals prior to wider implementation.

Final Recommendations

A year later, in September 1992, the City released its "Final Report and Recommendations-Housing on Toronto's Main Streets" which abandoned the phased approach. The three-phase implementation strategy was compressed into one phase, and the idea of using demonstrations areas to test the proposals was also dropped.

The City also settled for generalized built form provisions that were adopted on an area-by area basis, and site-specific rezoning would be used to determine the appropriateness of developments at higher densities.

Meanwhile, certain concerns about the proposals were emerging. The most significant related to the economic feasibility of large site redevelopment for social housing. Cityhome, Toronto's non-profit housing producer, was planning a prototype development at a site along Danforth Avenue, but a feasibility study of the project determined that its development in conformity with proposed zoning would result in a half million dollar shortfall.

Parking was another concern. The City's stringent parking standards were identified early in the program as a major disincentive to development, especially with regard to small sites. However, proposals to reduce parking standards and to give certain exemptions for small sites were of great concern to residents of adjacent neighbourhoods. Residents believed that these new standards would result in future parking problems on their streets. These concerns were shared by the City's Department of Public Works and Environment and the Parking Authority of Toronto.

Still other stakeholders, while supportive of the Main Streets concept, argued that the application of site-plan review to small scale development was a significant bureaucratic obstacle that would result in the program not achieving its stated goals and objectives.

Further Review and Fine-Tuning

The implementation strategy for Main Streets was reviewed by a team of external consultants. Their report, "Main Streets Review," completed in December 1992, called for a fast-tracked approvals process, exemptions for smaller properties, contextualized zoning to achieve a better physical fit with the street and adjacent neighbourhood, a process to create new lanes, and increased densities at transit nodes and landmark sites.

Few of the recommendations were incorporated into the January 1993 planning department report, "Fine-Tuning the Final Recommendations for Housing on Toronto Main Streets." Particularly contentious was the decision not to pursue a package of exemptions for smaller properties. The Main Streets Advocacy Group (MSAG), an independent organization committed to promoting the creation of "healthy, vibrant Main Streets", rejected the report stating that the interests of large scale housing producers were over-represented. MSAG instead urged the adoption of less stringent regulations for small sites.

The Ontario Ministry of Housing and the Toronto Society of Architects both complained that height limits were generally too low, that commercial parking standards were excessive, and that no provision was made for increased densities at subway nodes. The Confederation of Residents and Ratepayers Associations (CORRA), expressing the opposite view, stated that height limits were too high and that parking standards were too lenient. Meanwhile, the Toronto Historical Board continued in their call for appropriate incentives to encourage the preservation and rehabilitation of heritage properties on main streets.

The Final Proposals

Clearly a stalemate had developed over the implementation strategy for the Main Streets initiative. In acknowledgement of this situation, the City's Land Use Committee approved the broad Official Plan policies, but directed planners to establish a working committee composed of disgruntled stakeholders in hope of reaching a compromise position on the zoning package. The committee eventually reached a consensus which was presented to the Land Use Committee in July 22, 1993.

These proposals received unanimous approval. This latest package contains, among other things: a) an incentive package for small sites, including relaxed parking arrangements and exemption from site plan control; b) built form provisions which residents viewed as sensitive to adjacent neighbourhoods and existing streetscapes; c) special provisions for buildings of historic value, such as exemptions from parking and loading requirements and allowances for flexible use; d) permission for home occupations as an accessory use to residential floor space; and e) relief from new parking standards for retail and restaurant uses.

While all of this is good news for small site redevelopment, the bigger opportunities for Main Streets intensification seem to have been missed. The latest package contains no provision for higher levels of intensification around subway stations or at major intersections. Moreover, the two widest main streets in the city, St. Clair and Danforth Avenues, have had their building heights limited to approximately five storeys; arguably, both streets could have accommodated larger buildings. Moreover, the dropping of the phased implementation approach using demonstration areas and the abandonment of the Danforth site as a prototype project means the City has missed some superb opportunities to test and promote Main Streets intensification.

Bedford Glen:
A Designer's Role in Achieving Intensification

Leslie Coates

The study described here sets out to identify a successful intensification development and to find out why it works. What follows is an identification of the design features which contribute to the acceptance of Bedford Glen, a medium-density development located within a single-family neighbourhood in North Toronto. This study was funded in part by CMHC and was based on interviews with residents who live in the development, residents who live in the adjacent single-family neighbourhood and the project architect.

The Planning and Development of Bedford Glen

In 1965 a developer proposed building two massive towers within a predominantly single-family neighbourhood. By the mid-1970s the proposal was nearing collapse after years of battling local ratepayer groups and two OMB hearings. But the developer then tried a different approach. They embarked on a consultation process with the local community: a procedure which was at that time unique in Canada.

Within six months, a plan for the site had been approved and a Canadian Building headline declared: "Community participation in the design sells these homes before they're built." The 5.6 acre site remained the same. What had transpired was that the developer and local ratepayers' associations worked together to find a solution to their differences. They started by hiring architect Ernest Annau. Annau led the design team that included a community representative, and a developer representative. By 1979 the development was completed.

The project was called Bedford Glen and it stands as an example of a successful intensification project. While the density is less than proposed initially by the developer, it is almost twice that found in the adjacent residential area. Yet, both residents and neighbouring residents view Bedford Glen as an appropriate development and one that fits within the larger neighbourhood context. It was also judged a success in the marketplace as most of the project sold out before a single unit had been completed.

Organizing Principles: The Site Plan for Bedford Glen

Physically, the plan proposed by Annau Associates Architects Inc., was in marked contrast to what had been envisioned for the site. Unlike the towers that had been proposed, Bedford Glen is a low-rise, multiple housing development

Leslie Coates is a consultant in Toronto. She has a master's degree in landscape architecture from the University of Guelph, where she completed a thesis entitled *Factors Affecting the Acceptance of Higher Density Housing.*

Bedford Glen

made up of condominiums and town houses. The built-form solution for Bedford Glen was derived from the natural ravine setting that runs north to south through the site. While all other development scenarios had proposed filling in the ravine, architect Ernest Annau used this natural feature as an integral element in determining the layout and arrangement of buildings on the site.

Bedford Glen has a total of 207 units of housing. The masterplan breaks the

This map is quite interesting in its illustration of Bedford Glen within a single family neighbourhood.

residential development into small clusters consisting of two terraced buildings and a series of townhouses, which serve as a transition to the adjacent single-family neighbourhood. Parking is accommodated in underground garages for residents in the condominiums, and the townhouses have attached garages.

In the site layout the two terraced buildings trace the natural contours of the ravine and thus define the central landscaped space. This landscaped spine provides a distinct physical and visual

unifying element to which everything else relates. The terraced buildings have been sited so that a significant number of units face onto landscaped open space and each unit has private open space either in the form of a balcony or an at-grade patio. In the public open space of the development there is a waterfall which helps to attenuate the sound of nearby traffic.

Special attention was also given to connecting the new development with the surrounding neighbourhood. To achieve this, materials in keeping with those in the adjacent single-family houses were used. As well, the architect incorporated three pedestrian paths which connect the older community with the new one.

Factors Affecting the Acceptance of Higher Density Housing

The physical factors that contributed to the success of this development were its overall size, spacing of units, division into small clusters, facade design, visual and functional access to open space, private open space, privacy, and underground parking.

One objective of this study was to identify the features that neighbouring residents value in the Bedford Glen development. When asked what they like about Bedford Glen, neighbouring residents indicated the landscape design, visual appearance and design of the terraced buildings, absence of visible parking and the low-rise nature of the development.

While the density of the development had been a contentious issue at the outset, it no longer appears to concern neighbouring residents. When asked what they thought of the density, most neighbouring residents indicated that they did not find it dense. When asked why, they said: "human scale," "layout," "landscaping," "ravine setting," "people traffic minimal and not concentrated along any single path," "elevation differential," "cars seldom seen," "quiet atmosphere," and "well-kept grounds."

Integration with the Surrounding Community

The overall goal of Bedford Glen was to create a development which was physically and socially a part of the surrounding neighbourhood. When asked about this, neighbouring residents suggested that the development "fits in well." All neighbours agreed that a high-rise building would have been unacceptable.

Neighbouring residents were asked if they would consider moving to Bedford Glen in the future. Many neighbours indicated that this was a possibility. In the words of one neighbouring resident, "I might want to move to a condominium apartment type of housing and Bedford Glen would be the ideal because it is not a high-rise and when you are in there you feel you are part of the community around. The trees are pleasant and you feel close enough to the ground to see down below…I like the feel of it."

The importance of higher density developments appealing to the surrounding community cannot be overstated. If neighbouring residents find the design acceptable, it is less likely they will oppose it. Moreover, it is also possible that they will consider a move to the development if their own housing needs change. This study would indicate that for some neighbouring residents, Bedford Glen is a residential option for the future.

Lessons from Bedford Glen

As part of this study, residents of Bedford Glen and neighbouring residents were asked to comment on higher density developments in general and to evaluate a variety of developments within the medium-density range. Of particular interest was the general support voiced in favour of moderately higher densities as well as a willingness to entertain a range of intensification models.

The primary caution was what new developments might look like. While numerical density ranges meant little to neighbouring residents, they had no difficulty articulating what they liked or disliked about various schemes. When asked about how to implement intensification, they suggested that successful schemes be used as examples and that residents be given an opportunity to evaluate a range of designs. What they are asking for is in essence the very process by which Bedford Glen was created where a collaborative relationship was formed between the designer, the developer and the surrounding community - and one in which neighbouring residents had an opportunity to see and comment on a variety of design options, renderings and large-scale models of proposed schemes.

From this study, it appears that design plays an important role in shaping peoples' attitudes toward intensification, and a better understanding of how design can assist in making higher densities more palatable is vitally important in knowing how to build the housing to suit those requirements. Therefore, designers need to take the challenge to show the public what different densities can look like - and in so doing help to create a future in which an increase in density does not have to be regarded with fear and a sense of loss.

Woburn Avenue

Avenue Road

Site Plan for Bedford Glen

Greenwood Racetrack:
An Opportunity not to be Missed

Ken Greenberg

Ken Greenberg is a Principal with Berridge Lewinberg Greenberg Dark Gabor

When the Jockey Club decided to sell the Greenwood Racetrack site, it created a unique development opportunity right in the heart of the city. The future of this 82-acre site, situated next to the lake and within one of the most interesting and attractive neighborhoods in Toronto, will tell an important story about the kind of urban neighbourhoods we want to have in the GTA and how we are going to go about getting them.

For the past three decades, the expansion of the urban boundary of Toronto has proceeded largely unchecked. Only recently has public opinion and the emerging regional interest of the Provincial Government begun to recognize the real costs of sprawl: the loss of agricultural land, the excessive dependency on the automobile, and the loss of a genuinely diverse sense of community. There is a larger and less vocalized concern in this flight to edge cities for those who still live in the centre - that perhaps we are losing the ability to refresh and revitalize our own communities. The rapid changes in the structure of the urban economy, with the consequent abandonment of large obsolete sites, suggests that the need to find effective means of inner-city regeneration is urgent. We need to make the development of Greenwood a success in large part to demonstrate that we are not suffering from a collective lack of nerve in achieving the renewal essential for Toronto.

Creating a new community on the racetrack lands is the kind of challenge that we must collectively meet, not only because we desperately need attractive infill and intensification alternatives to the ubiquitous greenfield sprawl, but because after the collapse of Ataratiri and the blemished promise of Harbourfront, Toronto needs to show that it still knows how to make new places of excellent quality.

> The best parts of cities ... are... whole places, places in which housing, parks, stores and workplaces live harmoniously together.

As the planners of the site, it is important to appreciate that we personally have no specific preconception as to how it should be developed. Even though I have lived beside Greenwood for the past twenty-five years, it has only recently become for me anything other than a racetrack. We have to face this site with open minds, freshness, and imagination and let its own special characteristics, its particular 'genus loci' emerge. That is why we welcome the opportunity to work with a committee of local residents, because there is no monopoly of wisdom on trying to understand Greenwood's opportunities and complexities.

We are not naive about the deep concerns that many in the neighbourhood have about the development. There is an anxiety about change, exacerbated by the recession, that is quite understandable, especially given past experiences with redevelopment that has been harshly out of scale with the context of its surroundings. We are determined not to repeat those mistakes. The basic premise of the Greenwood development team is that whatever is created on the site must be based on the recognition and renewal of what is good and valid in the Beaches community.

What then is the best use of the site? Many have suggested that the area should be devoted exclusively to parkland. Frankly, I suspect this idea stems more from fears about the nature of possible development, than from a realistic appreciation of the consequences of a regional scale park at this location or from any honest reckoning of how the necessary financial resources to implement such a park could be found. Proposing such a park, in what is one of the most "parks rich areas" of the city, is to fail to meet the challenge of Greenwood, the challenge of finding ways, acceptable to the community, of repairing the large empty spaces created in the city fabric by obsolete uses.

We have to abandon the stark dichotomy of 'parkland' versus 'development' and realize that the best parts of cities, wonderfully exemplified by the Beaches, are whole places, places in which housing, parks, stores and workplaces live harmoniously together. This is not a revolutionary premise, rather it is a return to the best traditions of city building. We live in the modern era and our development will of necessity reflect our time, but it will be rooted in Toronto's well-tested experience about the mix and diversity that makes a good community.

Rather than a specific plan, we are coming to the site with a set of ideas, ideas that we want to work through with the local community to establish the principles for the development. Simply stated, these ideas are as follows:

• to create an interesting and attractive new neighbourhood within Toronto that people will want to visit, live and work in;

• to celebrate the wonderful natural and waterfront setting, with its parks, beaches and recreational attractions, making the necessary connections to the Martin Goodman trail, the boardwalk and to Queen St.;

• to explore the potential of utilizing 'green technologies' in servicing and other systems;

• to provide a neighbourhood that accommodates the new realities of working patterns and family lifestyles by offering flexible housing and workspaces and a range of different housing opportunities;

• to ensure in collaboration with the appropriate public agencies that the community facilities normally found in a neighbourhood of this scale, i.e., schools, local parks and neighbourhood services, are adequately provided; and,

• to deal with both locally generated and regional traffic demands to ensure, in collaboration with the City and Metro, that a good neighbourhood environment is created and no excessive demands are made on surrounding communities; the same thoughts go for parking provision.

Nothing radical or frightening in this list I hope. The challenge at Greenwood is to do the straightforward well, to creatively explore opportunities, to improve relationships and extend linkages, and to find the scale and complexity of community that makes it an asset and not a detriment to its neighbours. We have a lot of things going for us: a far-sighted developer with a commitment to quality; an extraordinary site; and a knowledgeable, if wary, local community. Toronto has to learn again how to make places of which it can be proud. If not here, where? If not now, when?

....

Exerpt from an article by John Barber,: the Globe & Mail, April 30, 1996.

"Boy, did we blow it. The Greenwood plan for new residential development by the lake ... is an abomination. It is so dreary, so primitive, so richly redolent of missed opportunity and failure. On the finest, most significant redevelopment site in greater Toronto, the city is preparing to commit a world-class embarassment".

Property Taxation and Urban Sprawl

Enid Slack

Enid Slack is
Principal of Enid
Slack Consulting
Inc.

This article is
adapted from *The
Land Use
Implications of
Alternative
Municipal
Financial Tools*,
prepared by the
author for the
Intergovernmental
Committee on
Urban and
Regional
Research
(ICURR).

In the July-August 1993 issue of the Intensification Report, Ron Kanter indicated that intensification had been inhibited, at least in part, by the financial practices of municipalities. This is probably true. To the extent that municipalities have made any connection between property taxes and land use, for example, the interest has centred largely on how to attract developments which bring lots of revenue to the municipality and require few services. There has been less concern, however, about how property taxes affect the location and density of development. The impact of property taxes, and financing tools more generally, on location and land use is extremely important: if a municipality is pursuing residential intensification and at the time same time is levying a tax that encourages urban sprawl, then the two policies are inconsistent.

What is the Impact of Property Taxes on Land Use?

To the extent that property taxes reflect the benefits received from local public services, they will be neutral with respect to development. In other words, if property taxes are clearly paying for services (e.g., such as water and sewers), then the decision about where to develop will be unaffected by the taxes: the taxes will be matched by the benefits received. When property taxes are not related to benefits, however, there will be an impact on the development decision.

Studies of the property tax conclude that the tax discourages development. Since the tax is levied on property values, any investment that will increase property values will make the property subject to a higher tax. This will be true for increases in the size of a building, investments in quality, and increases in density. In short, the property tax creates a disincentive to improve or increase the size of the build-

ing. Since the tax system results in higher effective tax rates on non-residential property than on residential property, commercial and industrial development are discouraged even more.

The property tax is based on property values, not on the benefits received from services. This means that some taxpayers will pay less in property taxes than they receive in services; others will pay more. To understand which types of developments are favoured under a property tax, consider a simple example of a circular city with three zones decreasing in density from the centre to the outlying area. Suppose that property values are highest in the central core and also that the costs of services decrease as density increases (this is probably true for "hard" services such as water and sewers but may not be for "soft" services such as welfare and education). In this example, then, the costs of services are highest in the outlying areas.

If properties in the municipality are assessed at market value, then central properties would be paying relatively more taxes than those in the outlying areas. Since it is assumed that the cost of services is relatively lower in the central area, the result is that properties in the central areas would be overcharged and properties in the outlying areas undercharged.

Suppose now that the assessment system is out of date and that the central area is relatively underassessed compared to outlying areas (as is the case in Metro Toronto, for example). Property taxes would be relatively lower in the central areas. In this case, central areas would pay relatively less taxes for relatively lower cost services, and outlying lower density areas would be paying relatively higher taxes for relatively more expensive services.

Under the current assessment system in Ontario, apartments are over-assessed relative to single-family homes. To the extent that the costs of services are lower in higher density developments, the current system favours single-family homes and discourages investment in apartments. Similarly, the assessment system discriminates against commercial and industrial properties as there is a differentially higher mill rate on commercial/industrial properties in municipalities and in most provinces. Again, to the extent that commercial/industrial properties use fewer services than residential properties, there is a disincentive to invest in commercial/industrial properties.

Suppose property taxes were based on something other than market value. The following examples show the impact of alternative property tax bases on development:

• A property tax based on front footage will provide an incentive to invest in properties with small front footage.

• A tax based on the square footage of buildings would discourage investments that increase the size of the building. Compared to a property tax based on market value, which discourages investment in all property improvements, a tax on the square footage of buildings would only discourage those investments that increased the size of the building.

• Relative to market value taxation, a tax based on the value of land in current use would reduce development pressure and discourage increases in density. By so doing, market value in current use would help to preserve farmland. Similarly for properties that are not in their most profitable use, the tax would not create an incentive for further development of the site.

• A property tax, based on the actual cost of replacement of improvements, would create an incentive to invest in less valuable structures and a disincentive to improve one's property.

• A site value tax, one that taxes only the land portion of property, would be neutral with respect to land use, assuming that land is in its most profitable use. There is no use of the land that would reduce the tax. A move from a property tax on land and buildings to a site value tax, however, would result in increased investment in building and improvements and increased intensity of land use. This result occurs because heavier taxation of land values increases the opportunity cost of holding land vacant and encourages more intensive uses.

In general, to the extent that the base of the tax reflects the use of local services, there will not be an impact on development decisions. However, where there is no direct relationship between the benefits received from local services and the property taxes paid, there will be an impact. Hence, heavier taxation of the improvements portion of the property will discourage more intensive uses; heavier taxation of the land portion of the property will encourage more intensive uses.

Should Tax Policy be Used to Achieve Land Use Objectives Such as Intensification?

The findings on property taxes indicate that property taxes can affect development decisions. Should they be used deliberately to influence these decisions? Consider an example where people value some open space more than the developer. If these positive societal benefits (externalities) are not considered by the developer, the land may be developed too quickly from the public's perspective. One way to alter the timing of development is to provide a subsidy to the developer which would increase the value of the land in its current use and provide an incentive to keep it in that use for a longer time. That subsidy could be in the form of lower rates of tax or lower assessed values for open space relative to other uses. Higher taxes on residential development will, other things being equal, discourage the developer from converting open space into a residential development.

... to the extent that the base of the tax reflects the use of local services, there will not be an impact on development decisions.

However, where there is no direct relationship between the benefits recieved from the local services and the property taxes paid, there will be an impact.

While it may be appropriate in theory to use tax policy to achieve land use objectives, it may be difficult in practice:

- Setting tax rates to achieve land use objectives requires knowing how much tax to charge. Even if this value could be determined, there may be situations where even reducing the tax to zero would not provide a sufficient incentive to alter land use decisions (e.g., preserve the open space).

- Land use objectives have changed significantly over the last thirty years from a desire to develop the urban fringe, to a desire for residential intensification and the preservation of open space. Throughout this period, however, it has been extremely difficult to change tax policy. For example, efforts to reform the property tax in some parts of Ontario have not

succeeded even after thirty years. Tax policy is a blunt instrument for achieving land use objectives.

- Local flexibility in tax policy (such as permitting municipalities to levy different tax rates on different types of property) may not solve the planning problems that are more regional or provincial in scope.

Conclusion

In summary, using tax instruments to implement land use objectives may simply not be effective. Given all of these constraints, it may not be appropriate to use the property tax to encourage intensification; it is also not appropriate, however, to have a property tax that discourages intensification. Tax policy should be designed to be at least neutral with respect to development decisions.

Sprout:
An Innovative Starter Home

Sevag Pogharian

Sevag Pogharian is President of Sevag Pogharian Design, a Montreal-based architectural firm specializing in housing.

Sprout is an innovative starter home designed to meet both the current constraints and needs of a young family while also anticipating its future needs. This innovative starter home-which is the result of work done under the aegis of Canada Mortgage and Housing Corporation's (CMHC) External Research Program1-makes homeownership more affordable for young families because, at its initial phase, it is very small (90 sq m of habitable area). Sprout starts off small since most young families neither need nor can afford a large house initially. As a

family's housing needs change and its financial means increase, however, Sprout's habitable area can be altered and expanded correspondingly. Sprout is designed to have the capacity to grow incrementally to keep up with the needs of a growing family. Through a series of alterations that can be made over time to meet a family's changing housing needs, Sprout's habitable area can be expanded up to three times its initial size to even accommodate an accessory apartment. Furthermore, unlike many traditionally designed houses, alterations can be made with minimal disruption to Sprout's existing structure and at minimal cost.

How is Sprout different from other affordable housing solutions?

Sprout improves upon two recently proposed solutions to the problem of affordable starter homes for young families-the Canadian Home Builders' Association (CHBA) / CMHC Demonstration Home known as Charlie and McGill University's Grow Home.

Charlie comprises a large two-storey structure with a full basement and a footprint of approximately 93 sq m. Charlie has, excluding its full basement, 186 sq m of habitable area. An innovative design feature of Charlie is its convertibility. In other words, this structure may comprise a single housing unit of 186 sq m or it may be converted into two smaller units of 93 sq m each. The proponents of Charlie suggest that a young family may buy this house, convert the second floor into a rental accessory apartment and use the rental revenue to offset monthly mortgage payments. Furthermore, the proponents suggest that when the family's housing needs expand, the family may reconvert Charlie into a single housing unit and appropriate the second floor for its own use.

The straightforward, low-tech flexibility built into the design of Charlie at the outset represents an intelligent and innovative approach to enhance affordability. This feature comprises Charlie's greatest strength while the specific design solution that embodies this approach has certain shortcomings. The most important shortcoming is that although a household may offset its monthly dwelling costs through converting the upper floor into an accessory apartment, the proponents of Charlie offer no solution to the potential hurdle represented by the required down-payment on a large house such as Charlie. Not surprisingly, therefore, CHBA's estimated minimum annual revenue for a couple to afford Charlie is $60,000 to $80,000. Charlie, therefore, is inaccessible to a major proportion of young Canadian families, i.e. those families earning less than $60,000 annually.

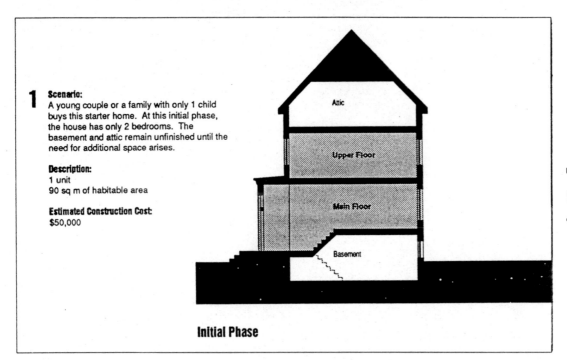

1 Scenario:
A young couple or a family with only 1 child buys this starter home. At this initial phase, the house has only 2 bedrooms. The basement and attic remain unfinished until the need for additional space arises.

Description:
1 unit
90 sq m of habitable area

Estimated Construction Cost:
$50,000

Attic
Upper Floor
Main Floor
Basement

Initial Phase

Initial Phase

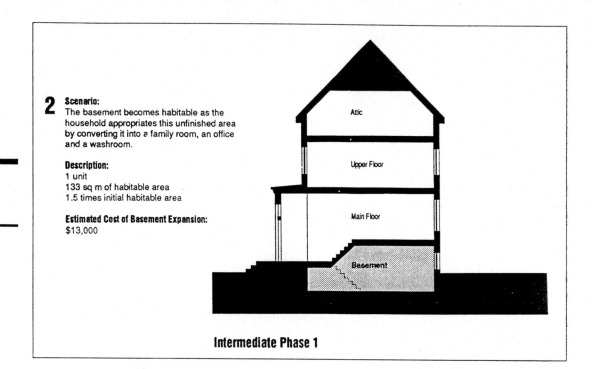

2 Scenario:
The basement becomes habitable as the household appropriates this unfinished area by converting it into a family room, an office and a washroom.

Description:
1 unit
133 sq m of habitable area
1.5 times initial habitable area

Estimated Cost of Basement Expansion:
$13,000

Intermediate Phase 1

The Grow Home, developed by McGill University's Affordable Homes Program, represents a different approach than Charlie's to achieving affordability. The objective underlying the Grow Home was to enhance affordability for first-time homebuyers by reducing the land and construction cost components associated with homebuilding. The approach to reducing these costs involved reducing the width, overall size, and complexity of the unit. The Grow Home concept was adopted by several homebuilders in the Montreal area and several hundred Grow Home-type units were built and sold in the region. This demonstrated that the strategy of reducing the overall size and complexity of a unit can successfully enhance affordability for first-time buyers.

A major shortcoming of the Grow Home, however, is that contrary to its name, it does not grow in any significant

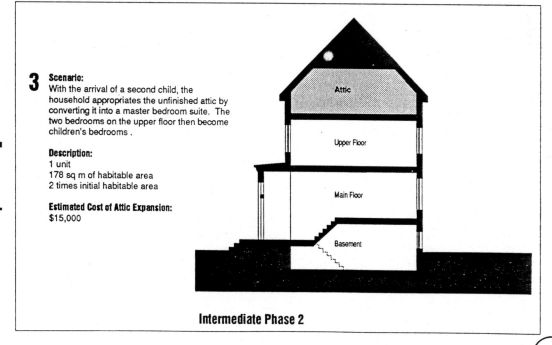

3 Scenario:
With the arrival of a second child, the household appropriates the unfinished attic by converting it into a master bedroom suite. The two bedrooms on the upper floor then become children's bedrooms .

Description:
1 unit
178 sq m of habitable area
2 times initial habitable area

Estimated Cost of Attic Expansion:
$15,000

Intermediate Phase 2

way. Expansion of its habitable space can only occur downward through finishing off the basement, where the unit has a basement. The opportunity of expanding upward into a habitable attic does not exist. Furthermore, expanding outward into the backyard through an addition is impossible due to the unit's layout as well as its condominium form of ownership. The unit in its townhouse typology cannot expand outward since this would result in a windowless bedroom at the upper floor. Moreover, because of zoning regulations in most municipalities in the Montreal Metropolitan area, the narrow 4.2 m width of the Grow Home has eliminated

which has negative consequences in terms of affordability. Furthermore, Sprout adopts the Grow Home's strategy of reducing unit size and complexity while overcoming the limitation of the Grow Home's unexpandability. Sprout can, therefore, enhance accessibility to home-ownership for young families as a result of its small initial size and consequent low land and construction costs. It can also offer its occupants the opportunity of modifying and expanding the house to suit their changing housing needs. Sprout's layout and freehold form of ownership permit the occupants to expand the habitable area downward into the basement, upward into the attic, and

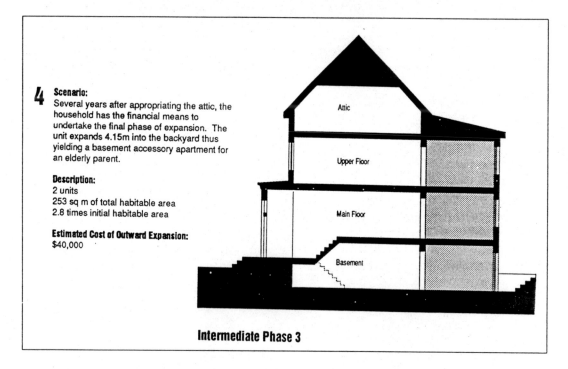

4 Scenario:
Several years after appropriating the attic, the household has the financial means to undertake the final phase of expansion. The unit expands 4.15m into the backyard thus yielding a basement accessory apartment for an elderly parent.

Description:
2 units
253 sq m of total habitable area
2.8 times initial habitable area

Estimated Cost of Outward Expansion:
$40,000

Attic

Upper Floor

Main Floor

Basement

Intermediate Phase 3

freehold as a tenure option. Grow Home-type units in the Montreal region have sold exclusively as condominiums-a form of ownership that prohibits building additions.

Sprout shares certain positive design features with the above precedents while rejecting those features that have negative consequences. Sprout adopts Charlie's valid strategy of building into a new house, right from the beginning, adequate design reserve to allow future conversions. However, it rejects Charlie's large size

outward through an addition. Sprout's design flexibility also provides its occupants the possibility of an eventual accessory apartment. Furthermore, the conversions that Sprout can undergo are designed to occur with minimal disruption to the existing structure and at minimal cost.

Potential benefits of Sprout

Though not the panacea for all housing problems, this innovative housing type can respond to several important issues facing Canadian municipalities and young housing consumers.

Over the past few decades, the downtown household population of many urban municipalities has declined as households-particularly young families-have moved to the suburbs in search of housing that better meet their needs. The elements driving the exodus of families to the suburbs involve easier access to homeownership, the desire for private outdoor space, privacy, and the possibility of adapting the house as the family evolves.

In order to reverse the exodus of young families to the suburbs, many municipalities are attempting to expand, within downtown neighborhoods, the supply of residential choices commensurate with the means, needs and aspirations of young prospective homebuying families. Sprout offers this segment of homebuying families many of the elements that appear to be drawing them to the suburbs. Thus, Sprout, as a housing type, may benefit urban municipalities by helping reduce the tide of young families toward the suburbs.

Sprout represents a housing product that lends itself to both small and large infill developments. Developing infill lots with products such as Sprout would gradually increase a municipality's density. Densification signals more efficient use of existing infrastructure and resources as well as an increase in the municipality's tax base. Furthermore, as Sprout's habitable space is increased by its occupants, a municipality would enjoy tax benefits through the increased assessment value of the property.

Sprout's inherent flexibility and design reserve provide a household with many choices. A household can readily modify Sprout to accommodate its changing housing needs. These changing needs may involve an additional bedroom, a family room, a home office or even an accessory apartment. Sprout's malleability and capacity to respond to changing housing needs means that a household can stay in the same house and neighbourhood for a long time. Thus,

Sprout's inherent design reserve can enhance the stability of neighborhoods and communities.

Sprout can fit many different stylistic contexts thus reinforcing the architectural tradition of its neighborhood rather than disrupting it. Sprout's main facade can easily adopt the local vocabulary and materials whether this means gray limestone and bay-windows, or cedar shingles and clapboard siding. Furthermore, Sprout does not disrupt the character of a neighborhood as it grows and changes since the modifications that the dwelling undergoes do not become manifest on its main facade or building height.

The accessory apartments that can be created within Sprout would be of high quality in terms of health and safety. Many of the accessory apartments illustrated in the mentioned report have two means of egress and ample fenestration. Furthermore, all the illustrated accessory apartments comply fully with National Building Code 1990 requirements. Sprout's capacity to expand and easily accommodate an accessory apartment can have profound financial and lifestyle implications for a home owner. A home owner may create an accessory apartment and rent it out, thus, using the rental revenue to cover household expenses. Or, a home owner may make the accessory apartment available to an elderly parent, thus, creating a mutually beneficial extended family arrangement.

The next step

The positive reaction to Sprout, to-date, from the general public affirms that this innovative starter home has design merit and a potential market. Hence, we are now working towards realizing a demonstration project featuring two Sprouts.

Editor's note: This demonstration project was located in Montreal at McGill University from spring of 1995 to the fall of 1996.

Industrial Lands Strategy: City of Vancouver Draws the Line

Christina DeMarco

Planning policy on intensification generally focuses on means of increasing people and/or housing density in established and new areas. Converting underutilized industrial areas to new residential areas has been seen as an effective way of intensifying. It is an easy policy to implement - development is achieved without imposing much change in established neighbourhoods.

In Vancouver successful residential communities have been built on former industrial land. From the mid-1970s to 1990, about 700 acres of industrial land were rezoned. Before releasing any additional industrial lands, the City of Vancouver recently undertook a comprehensive review of the role and function of its remaining industrial lands. This article outlines the findings of the review and how Vancouver's industrial land policy relates to intensification objectives.

Work as a City Shaper

Work to a large extent shapes the city. Private transport has freed both job location and home location. Intensification policies therefore need to consider the mosaic of land uses which make up a complete community - not just housing.

When evaluating the performance of industrial activity in relation to intensification objectives, there are three key issues:

• Is industry using city land efficiently?

• Does industrial activity enhance access by proximity?

• What are the competing demands for other uses and what contribution would they make to intensification?

Industrial Land: Efficient Use of City Land?

About 1,700 acres, or six per cent of the City's land area, remains in industrial zoning. There are 2,000 firms and 46,500 jobs located on these lands. Unlike east-

ern markets, the industrial land market in Vancouver is buoyant. Vacancy rates for industrial space are less than five per cent region-wide and less than eight per cent in the city. Good, efficient space is easily rented. New construction as well as renovation is occurring at many locations in the industrial areas.

Industrial areas in close proximity to downtown help enable downtown areas to achieve their high densities. For example, restaurants do not have to have large food storage capacity with food wholesalers so close at hand. This is also true for office supplies, report and archive storage, among others.

Many industrial areas in the city have employment densities of 100 workers to the acre. When city industrial jobs move out to the suburbs they consume much more land - industrial densities in the City are over three or four times the worker and floorspace densities as suburban industrial development.

Enhancing Access by Proximity

The City of Vancouver and the Greater Vancouver Regional District (GVRD) have a policy of "planning by proximity" which seeks to minimize the demand for movement through the convenient arrangement of land uses. The degree to which maintaining industrial land in the City meets this objective can be measured by two criteria:

1   the extent to which industries that are located in the City serve its businesses and residents, and

2   the extent to which City industry employs City residents.

1. City Serving Industry

The nature of industry has changed dramatically over the last twenty years. Sawmills, metal fabricators, and large wholesalers have moved out. Only about 14 per cent of industry remaining in the city can be classified as traditional indus-

Christina DeMarco is a planner in the City Plans Division of the Vancouver Planning Department. Prior to joining the City of Vancouver she worked for ten years in Austrailia on metropolitan planning for Sydney, Canberra, and Perth. She is the author of two books: *Planning Sydney's Future* and *On a Human Scale: A Life in City Design*.

try. Today's businesses locate in the City for two key reasons: it is the best place to serve their customers, and it offers some sort of comparative advantage such as proximity to the port or labour force. Small manufacturers, service industries, building maintenance, machine and auto repair, import/exporters, etc. are typical users of industrial space.

About 50 per cent of the businesses located in industrial areas have been at their present location for less than seven

Vancouver had retained approximately 1700 acres of designated industrial land in 1995, compared to about 2400 acres in 1973.

efficient servicing of downtown and port functions.

2. Employment of City Residents by Industry

The journey to work by car continues to create a large demand for urban land. Despite the declining proportion of work trips as a percentage of total trips, road infrastructure is still designed around peak period demands. Car-dependent work trips also create other car-depend-

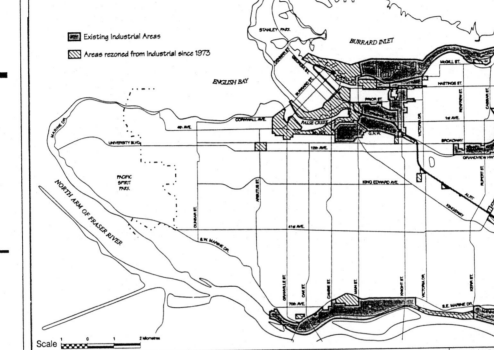

Existing Industrial Areas

Areas rezoned from Industrial since 1973

Industrial Areas in Vancouver

City of Vancouver Planning Department

date: April 1995
by: CD/dem
scale: 1:100000

years. City industry sells 70 per cent of all goods and services sold in the Lower Mainland to customers located within the City. For supplies, City industry receives 60 per cent from other City firms. One industry operator referred to the industrial areas as the "refrigerator, storeroom, and repair room of the downtown." By having these functions close at hand there is less need for road space for both goods movement and service trips.

The city-serving nature of industry has important consequences for intensification. The convenient arrangement of service and suppliers means less pressure on transportation infrastructure and

ent trips, i.e., the trip from the business park to the shopping mall for lunch. Another means of promoting intensification is to encourage the use of transit for the journey to work. This can be more easily achieved when workers live close to work.

About two-thirds of resident blue-collar workers work in a job located in the City. The City of Vancouver, and more specifically the eastside, still has the highest concentration of blue-collar resident workers in the region. In fact the number of blue-collar workers residing in the city increased by seven per cent between 1986 to 1991 to 56,000. In many neighbourhoods on the eastside, one third of resident workers are employed in blue-collar trades.

In the City of Vancouver, 24 per cent of industrial workers get to work by transit, nine per cent walk, and eight per cent go by bicycle. By way of comparison, in Richmond, the neighbouring suburban municipality on the southside of the City, five per cent of the industrial workers take transit, two per cent take bikes, and nobody walks.

The good match between home and work is partly explained by the migrant-receiving role the City continues to play. The east side of the City not only has a stock of blue-collar jobs but also a stock of affordable rental housing and a good public transit system. For entrepreneurs and employees alike, the east side provides the "first rung of the ladder" conditions.

If the industrial job base is lost to the suburbs, there is likely to be a spatial mismatch between workers and jobs. A high proportion of the workers will continue to live in the City where rental costs are lower. Their commute out to a new job will mean longer trips and will probably require a car.

Balancing Competing Demands for Industrial Land

Practically all of the City's industrial land makes for good housing land. In the present market, there is considerable pressure to convert industrial land to housing.

Vancouver presently has a large unbuilt capacity of condominium space within walking distance of the downtown. In the case of converting virtually vacant industrial land to housing within walking distance to the downtown, there were clearly considerable intensification gains. However, the remaining industrial lands are occupied by firms largely serving the City and employ a high proportion of City workers. For the remaining parcels of industrial land there is likely to be little or no improvement in the jobs/housing balance by converting industrial land to housing land.

Views from a broad cross-section of the community were canvassed to determine what value the community placed on industrial activity remaining in the City. The CityPlan program was running in tandem with the industrial lands review and provided an opportunity to gauge citizens' views on the alternate uses of industrial land. Through the "Futures" stage of CityPlan, citizens were shown the consequences of four alternate futures. The alternative of using all industrial lands for housing was depicted as well as futures which retained existing industrial land. The future which released industrial land for housing offered the community a chance to intensify without impacting their neighbourhoods. To do this they had to accept less job diversity and services. The community chose to protect industrial lands and opted for a future that intensified residential, retail, and office development around

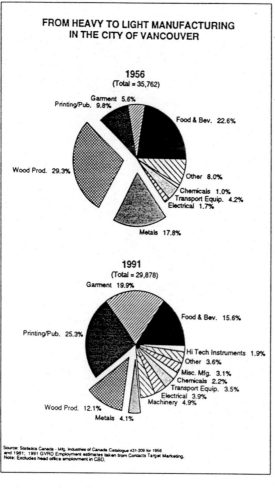

FROM HEAVY TO LIGHT MANUFACTURING
IN THE CITY OF VANCOUVER

1956
(Total = 35,762)

Garment 5.6%
Printing/Pub. 9.8%
Food & Bev. 22.6%
Other 8.0%
Chemicals 1.0%
Transport Equip. 4.2%
Electrical 1.7%
Wood Prod. 29.3%
Metals 17.8%

1991
(Total = 29,878)

Garment 19.9%
Printing/Pub. 25.3%
Food & Bev. 15.6%
Hi Tech Instruments 1.9%
Other 3.6%
Misc. Mfg. 3.1%
Chemicals 2.2%
Transport Equip. 3.5%
Electrical 3.9%
Machinery 4.9%
Wood Prod. 12.1%
Metals 4.1%

Source: Statistics Canada - Mfg. Industries of Canada Catalogue #31-209 for 1956 and 1981; 1991 GVRD Employment estimates taken from Contacts Target Marketing.
Note: Excludes head office employment in CBD.

existing neighbourhood centres. This finding was also confirmed through public input on the draft Industrial Lands Strategy.

Protecting Industrial Areas Through Zoning

Following extensive public review of the draft policy, in March 1995 City Council supported the Planning Department recommendations and voted to retain the existing industrial areas.

What kind of policy is needed to keep the industrial lands viable? There are two key features of the policy: keep industrial land for industry; and, be stringent on rezoning requests.

One of the biggest threats to a viable central city industrial base is the cost of land and rents. The Strategy recommends that industrial areas remain exclusively industrial, with retail and office as ancillary uses only. On the face of it, this goes against vibrant mixed use zoning. But the reality is that if the City does in fact want to retain any industrial areas it has to protect them from higher rent uses such as artist live-work studios, and retail and office units. The industrial areas are walking distance to commercial strips and residential neighbourhoods. In fact many restaurant and shop owners noted that they depend on nearby industrial workers as customers.

While residents want shops and cafes nearby they are not particularly interested in auto body repair shops, or warehouses with truck deliveries throughout the night. Industry operators are happy to be surrounded by similar types of industry to avoid resident complaints.

Rezoning criteria in the Industrial Lands Strategy are stringent. The Strategy states that rezonings will only be considered in the context of a City-initiated area plan. Predictions are that if the Strategy policies are followed, then industrial land prices are likely to fall. With about 66 per cent of the industry operators being tenants, that is good news for the future of the industry in the City.

Conclusion

Maintaining existing industry can make an important contribution to intensification. Intensification objectives, however, are not the only planning objectives to be considered in maintaining and creating complete communities. In the case of industry, the retention of jobs also makes good sense in terms of economic vitality and equity. With jobs so difficult to create, it seems prudent to hold onto existing jobs, especially high value added jobs. Letting go of industrial land is almost always a one way street; it is unlikely that it can ever be returned once it is rezoned. In terms of equity, Vancouver's diverse population profits from conserving the central structure and variety of a growing metropolis and having a choice of jobs, public transit, and affordable housing within easy reach.

The City of Vancouver has a population of almost 500,000 and about 300,000 jobs. It has about 27 percent of the region's population and 37 percent of its jobs. It has about one third of the industrial floorspace of the region.

Quantitative Risk Assessment for Contaminated Sites: A Tool for Intensification

Scott MacRitchie

Scott MacRitchie is a Toronto based Environmental Consultant and Hydrogeologist who works on resource protection strategies and urban issues such as redevelopment of contaminated lands.

Sucessful implementation of intensification and redevelopment policies requires the clean up of municipal industrial lands that are currently vacant, but may be contaminated. There is some concern that stringent clean-up levels will make it impossible to profitably redevelop a contaminated site for a sensitive land use such as housing. What is needed is a method that determines clean-up levels that are protective of public health and the environment and that are financially viable. Quantitative risk assessment has the potential to meet these needs once its subjective aspects have been recognized and dealt with. But how can it be quantitative and subjective? How can its subjective aspects be dealt with? If quantitative risk assessment is to be used as a tool for intensification, then these questions must be addressed. The following article is based on preliminary research conducted to address these questions.

Background on Quantitative Risk Assessment (QRA)

Due to the complexity of soil contamination and the pressing need to deal with it (Sheppard et al., 1992), a number of methods have been developed to determine concentrations of contaminants in soils that will not harm public health or the environment.

Attention and controversy has focused on two approaches to determining clean-up levels (Gaudet et al., 1992; Sheppard et al., 1992; Wong et al., 1991). The first approach is the generic or absolute approach, which is a relatively simple list of the maximum concentrations of contaminants in soils that will not harm human health or the environment. The generic approach does not account for site-specific or socio-economic factors.

The second approach is quantitative risk assessment (QRA), which has been used to determine clean up levels in British Columbia and is part of the national guidelines for decommissioning industrial sites of the Canadian Council of Ministers of the Environment (CCME, 1991). It is also one of three options for determining clean-up levels in the Proposed Guidelines for the Clean Up of Contaminated Sites in Ontario along with background levels and generic lists of levels (MOEE, 1994).

There are clear advantages to QRA over the generic approach. The QRA approach determines customized clean-up levels for each site that may maximize clean-up efficiency and minimize costs (Gaudet et al., 1992). QRA forces the integration of information about a site which leads to a better understanding of the problem and provides a process for choosing possible solutions (Wong et al., 1991). The result is a more efficient clean-up program that reduces costs (Petito Boyce and Michelsen, 1993) and maximizes protection to site workers, future users, and the environment. The great advantage of QRA

over the generic approach is its ability to take into account site-specific factors, which can greatly influence the risk posed by contaminants.

Subjectivity of QRA

There are problems and limitations with quantitative risk assessment that could severely restrict or impede its successful application. Stages and elements of QRA not only contain high degrees of uncertainty and variability, but have been criticised for being subjective and laden with value judgements.

Assumptions and sometimes judgements must be made to address uncertainty and variability. Health risk assessments often use incidence of cancer as an indicator of risk to health. This may seem reasonable since cancer is often fatal, but it is not the only disease or dysfunction that can occur due to exposure to environmental contamination. The Director of the Center for Risk Analysis of the Harvard School of Public Health has written (Warner North et al., 1991: 37):

> ... some citizens may be deluded into thinking that comparative risk analysis is a purely scientific undertaking. It is not. Risk assessment, while useful, cannot usually offer policy makers a high degree of precision. The more fundamental point is that judgements must be made about tradeoffs between cherished values, such as protection of public health and preservation of ecosystems. Even within the domain of human health, value judgements must be made about the relative importance of cancer and noncancer health effects (e.g., neurological effects).

In an issue of *Environmental Professional* devoted to risk assessment, Donald A. Brown of the Pennsylvania Department of Environmental Resources writes (Brown, 1992: 185):

> Often, important ethical or values decisions are hidden in what appear to be value-neutral risk assessment calculations ... Because of extensive scientific uncertainty in animal to

What is needed is a method that determines clean-up levels that are protective of public health and the environment and that are financially viable.

human extrapolations and fate and transport modeling of exposure pathways, risk assessors must make assumptions which oversimplify the "real world" conditions. Often these assumptions are conservative, and therefore environmentally protective. Usually these assumptions must be made in part on ethical or policy reasons; consequently, the risk assessment is rarely "ethically neutral," despite "value-free" pretensions of risk assessors.

The work of Brunk et al. (1991) used the registration cancellation of the herbicide alachlor as a case study to investigate the normative assumptions in QRA. The three different parties that conducted risk assessments on the herbicide -the Health Protection Branch of Health and Welfare Canada, the manufacturer, and the Alachlor Review Board, produced exposure estimates that ranged from 0.0000009 to 2.7 mg/kg of body weight per day. Brunk et al. (1991) found that different interpretations and assumptions by the three parties at all stages of the risk assessment process produced results that differed by over six orders of magnitude (i.e., one million). In their conclusion they state that:

> The debate concerning alachlor's risk to its users and to the Canadian public, as well as the question of the acceptability of that risk, is not a purely scientific, to say nothing of a value-free or socially neutral, enterprise. It is an intrinsically political debate among the various value communities (e.g., industry, farmers, environmentalists, farm-wives, etc.). (Brunk et al., 1991: 151)

Dealing with Subjectivity in QRA

The evidence suggests that, although QRA uses the tools of science, it is not itself a science because of its value judgements. The next question to be addressed then is whose values should be used in making these judgements. Very little has been written about how to deal with the problem of value judgements in risk assessment. Shrader-Frechette (1990: 39)

looks at the role of expert judgement in determining environmental risk and states that risk assessment and management needs to be reformed in at least three ways:

1. Instead of having experts perform a single study, we need to develop different approaches, weighting them on the basis of different value systems and different value judgements.

2. We need to debate merits of alternative analysis, each with its own interpretational and evaluative weights. Citizens can decide not only what policy they want, but also what value systems they wish to guide these decisions.

3. We need to weight expert opinion on the basis of past predictive successes.

Shrader-Frechette (1990: 40) goes on to say that the above reforms are subject to changes in perspective of risk assessment. Practitioners of risk assessment must give up the "...naive positivist assumption that expert assessments are wholly objective and value free..." and that "...contemporary technology/risk assessment needs to become more democratic, more open to control by the public, and more responsive to populist accounts."

To deal with public perception of risk, a whole new discipline of risk communication has developed which, according to Renn (1992: 467), seeks to "expose the target audience to a system of meaningful signals, which in turn may change their perception of the issue or their image of the sender." Lynn (1990) has examined the role of the public in environmental decision making and suggests that not only has the public a "right-to-be informed" (a purpose of risk communication) but a "right to know and to generate knowledge." She states that:

> The next steps entail ensuring that the public is involved in defining the parameters of the problem, framing questions to be answered, deciding what information needs to be generated, interpreting the information, and choosing among public policy

Often, important ethical or value decisions are hidden in what appears to be value-neutral risk assessment calculations ...

options and means of implementation. For risk managers the challenge is to give public participation plans and activities the same priority and resources as technical studies. (Lynn, 1990: 101)

Indeed, this has been recognized in the National Guidelines for Decommissioning Industrial Sites produced by the Canadian Council of Ministers of the Environment (CCME, 1991). In the section on development of clean-up criteria, the role of interested parties and other factors is discussed and the following conclusion is made:

Factors such as these, though not scientific or technical in nature, can play as large a role in the establishment of clean-up criteria as more scientific aspects. Regulatory agencies must remain responsive to the different sensitivities, priorities, and perspectives that interested parties bring to the process of developing environmental guidelines. (CCME, 1991: 49)

Conclusion

The public needs to be involved in the process by which risk assessment and management is formulated. A modified QRA process would allow public input in the selection of parameters that involve value judgements such as hazard identification, receptor characteristics (adult, child, flora, fauna), exposure pathways (inhalation, ingestion, dermal contact) and management options, to name a few. This process will facilitate direct communication between affected parties and will lead to a better understanding of risk and the risk assessment process among the public.

The exciting challenge is to create a process where lay people and experts can work together toward a common goal while respecting each other's perspectives and opinions. The anticipated benefit is to achieve a broader public consensus on environmental risk and clean-up levels while increasing the viability of remediating contaminated lands in order to promote intensification. Quantitative risk assessment can be a tool for intensification if it is made open and accessible to the public.

Greenbelt Alliance on Infill Housing

Greenbelt Alliance of the San Francisco Bay Area

Greenbelt Alliance is the Bay Area's citizen land conservation and urban planning organization. Known for opposing sprawl development, we also work to promote its alternatives, including "infill development."

What is infill development?

Infill is building homes, businesses and public facilities on unused and under-utilized lands within existing urban areas. Infill development keeps resources where people already live and allows rebuilding to occur. Infill development is the key to accommodating growth and redesigning our cities to be environmentally and socially sustainable.

Does infill provide more housing options?

Absolutely. These days we are seeing smaller families with working and single parents, singles of all ages, and people wanting work spaces in their homes. This

This article is reprinted from the Web site of the Greenbelt Alliance of the San Francisco Bay Area.

diversity of needs is often overlooked by development built exclusively for the 1950's-style family (working dad and domestic mom) which now accounts for only 14% of U.S. households (see below). Inill can encourage a variety of designs and housing options - second units, town houses, bungalows, studios, and cohousing - which are closer to jobs and services and less expensive than oversized housing at the urban fringe.

Will infill bring low-income housing projects to my neighborhood?

Not necessarily, but we still need to provide housing opportunities for all kinds of people. Instead of huge housing projects, proponents of infill often recommend a mix of market-rate and affordable housing. As in the natural world, achieving balance and diversity in our communities is healthy and creates richer experiences in the places we live.

Will higher density increase crime?

No! No study has ever established a link between crime increases and housing density. In fact, density and design can enhance safety by ensuring visibility and creating a sense of community through natural interactions and shared spaces.

Will higher density crowd our cities and worsen traffic congestion?

All growth increases traffic, but infill can alleviate congestion by reducing trips and encouraging alternative transportation.

Good infill projects are sometimes "mixed-use," placing residences and businesses in close proximity. Bringing homes and jobs together, along with services like shopping, schools and recreation, shortens trips and makes walking and bicycling more appealing.

Only higher housing densities can support transit like light rail. A major study found that in a neighborhood with 15 homes per acre, one-third fewer auto trips occur compared to a suburban tract. The bottom line is that infill is necessary for giving us transportation choices beyond the automobile.

What does infill development mean for children?

Infill can be a boon for children, creating safe opportunities for play and discovery. As infill offers more transit options and closer destinations, teenagers will not be entirely dependent on their parents for transportation. Of course, successful infill designs will be attentive to a variety of special needs and enhance the lives of all people, old as well as young.

How do infill's costs add up?

Without doubt, infill development is less expensive than sprawl in the long run. However, because of up-front costs, building within the city is often less profitable to the developer, who pays for site cleanup, zoning permits, building on a small scale, and accommodating neighborhood concerns.

But according to the Urban Land Institute, urban sprawl eventually costs from 40-400% more than infill development due to the costs of building and maintaining new roads, sewers, fire stations and schools, not to mention the health and psychological costs of air pollution, traffic congestion and loss of open space. The costs of sprawl are passed on to communities as higher taxes, the deterioration of local businesses, and a declining quality of life.

What can I do to encourage infill?

A great deal. Citizen participation is important in the rebuilding process. You can work with Greenbelt Alliance on a variety of pro-city projects, which include:

Awareness and education; Endorsements of appropriate compact housing proposals; and Policy research and partnership development.

... density and design can enhance safety by ensuring visibility and creating a sense of community through natural interactions and shared spaces.

Tackling Superstore Sprawl

John Weiler

Superstores have earned the epithet "non-place retailing" because of their lack of aesthetic appeal, but for preservationists, there's a lot more at stake - important economic, social and environmental issues. Supersprawl represents a crucial round in the flight for the future of Main Street, a battle in which Heritage Canada and others have been embroiled since the late 1970s. It could bring the knock-out blow for older downtowns already in trouble with serious repercussions for the civilizing qualities of urban living.

The historical roots of this threatening development are clear. Since the end of World War II we have been progressively building a new type of city - the low density suburb, and with it a novel approach to retailing - the shopping plaza. Fuelled by our love affair with the automobile and our passion for convenience - wanting everything closer, faster and, of course, cheaper - we drove the suburb out of control. We've not only gone through various stages of urban sprawl, but beyond to the current mania for edge cities. Retailing simply shifted gears. Local suburban shopping plazas gradually gave way to regional shopping centres - multipurpose suburban hubs - and, in turn, these are losing out to their logical successor, the big box.

Superstore economics is fairly basic. Retailers capture a bigger share of the value added to a product during the distribution stage, keep capital costs to minimum and rely on high volume, no-frills and low margins. Essentially, they cut out the distribution and wholesale functions and deal directly with manufacturers. This retailing revolution is also made possible by advanced technology for data collection and pricing goods (e.g., bar coding), that allows for combined cash flow management and inventory control.

Nevertheless, the private gain of the superstores comes at a cost to the public, far greater than the price of things bought in these temples of consumerism. The harm that big boxes bring is getting high profile attention in the United States and Britain. Recent developments surrounding the National Trust for Historic Preservation in the U.S. and a U.K. House of Commons Environment Committee, respectively, serve as useful touchstones for Canadians. By comparison, our public policy debate on superstores is just getting off the ground, and preservationists need all the help they can get.

In the United States, seedbed of the superstore phenomenon, only a few places are staring down the big box chain stores. Wal-Mart, the world's largest retailer, is still growing. It and similar chains are building new stores ranging from 50,000 to 200,000 square feet or more. Even if one community rejects a big chain, the chances are good that it will try to locate nearby, simply by going to the next interchange, in another municipal jurisdiction.

Even so, Americans are not taking it lying down. The 1995 New Year's Day edition of *The Washington Post*, in its annual list of what's hot and what's not, said "sprawl" is OUT and "Main Street" is IN. The weapon of first choice against the superstore is strong regional planning. Vermont, whose Act 250 allows environmental reviews of projects with regional impacts, is the only state in the nation without a Wal-Mart, although two proposals are pending. In Massachusetts, the Cape Cod Commission has blocked a warehouse megastore proposal, citing heavy traffic impacts, water usage and degradation of community character. All the same, such developments are the exception; most often, local governments are left to face the big boxes with zoning codes and negotiation.

The National Trust for Historic Preservation has stepped into the fray as a nationwide coordinator of activity and information exchange for superstore "sprawlbusters". Constance Beaumont, director of state and local policy and the

John Weiler, Vice-President (Research and Development) of Heritage Canada, has particular expertise in preservation planning.

Trust, based in Washington D.C., says that her organization sees superstores as a distinct new phase in supersprawl, one with serious consequences.

Last year, Ms. Beaumont wrote a guide published by the Trust called, *How Superstore Sprawl Can Harm Communities and What Citizens Can Do About It.* The guide focusses on three major harmful impacts - scale, location and design. Specific adverse effects include:

- saps the lifeblood of main street by shifting the concentration of retail activity to highway interchanges on the edge of town;

- displaces existing businesses, especially independently owned ones;

- may drive up state income taxes because big boxes are costly to service - roads, water and sewer, police, and other public services;

- causes waste or abandonment of previous public and private investments in established retailing areas; and,

- results in the homogenization of the country, since stores have no relation to their surroundings.

In proposing solutions, the Trust seeks to balance preservation principles with the mainstream of American values and behaviour. It recognizes that retailing changes and global economic forces cannot be controlled, and that it is almost impossible to hold back Americans' desire for low prices and convenience. The principal thrust of the Trust's publication is to point out that corporate retailers and communities have choices in dealing with the superstore.

The choices favoured by the Trust are twofold. Locate superstores in existing cities and towns. And, build stores that harmonize with the surroundings or better still, recycle disused older buildings. The guide defines the term "sprawl", reveals the public policies and private practices that encourage it, catalogues the adverse effects of superstore sprawl, and gives a common scenario for

the aggressive tactics used by big box promoters. Next, the Trust lays out fifteen strategies for curtailing the retailing colossus; sets fourteen commandments for dealing with the media; features four case studies of communities that have successfully fended off superstores; and, highlights good examples of alternatives - downtown revitalization schemes, adaptive use of older structures, and better models of new superstore designs.

With the guide, the National Trust for Historic Preservation has made a major contribution to the public policy debate over the superstore. But it has not stopped there. In March 1995, for instance, it co-sponsored with the Brookings Institutions and the Lincoln Institute, a national forum entitled, Alternatives to Sprawl.

Meanwhile, some interesting things have been happening across the Atlantic. With its old cities, rural traditions and tough planning laws, Britain did not experience huge suburban stores and their parking lots until the mid 1980s. Now, the superstore is well on its way. Thurrock Lakeside (opened in 1992), east of London, is one of the two or three largest in the U.K. It's a 1.2 million square foot shopping mall that includes department stores and space for 250 other retailers. The nearby town has paid the price. Many storefronts are empty in the old town centre, where even the venerable Marks & Spencer has closed.

Spurred by public concern and pleas for guidance from local authorities, the Department of the Environment, which is responsible for planning and conservation, got the Government to strike a House of Commons Committee to look into the matter. The Committee report, *Shopping Centres and Their Future*, was widely praised by conservation organizations, especially the prestigious Civic Trust.

The report signalled concern about the increasing developer interest in small towns, as most retailers shift their attention from largely saturated markets in metropolitan areas and cities. Committee members' key recommendation was that the Government amended policy guidance under British planning legislation to

A retailing juggernaut confronts cities and towns on both sides of the Atlantic. It's called the superstore or big box or simply, the "out-of-town" retail store. Typically, superstores locate at major highway interchanges in the suburban fringe and are surrounded by acres of parking. Often, several of these warehouse-style monsters set up shop in an open plaza known as a power centre or retail park. In North America, major trend setters include Wal-Mart, CostCo, Price Club and Home Depot.

include a clear presumption that superstores be located in or on the very edge of town centres unless there are strong indications to the contrary. The report also said that no proposals for superstores or other large retail developments, in or near small towns, should be considered unless they are accompanied by a comprehensive study of the possible retail effects over the whole of the proposal's catchment area.

There were several other recommendations worth highlighting. The Committee called for automatic review by the Minister of the Environment of superstore proposals that depart from statutory local plans. It also recommended more powers be given to local planners to deal with predatory trading practices of retail warehouse parks and price clubs. The Committee report asked as well that requirements for environmental impact assessment studies supplement planning regulations. And, the report stressed the need for better integration between transport and land-use planning to handle traffic problems and to encourage good-quality parking.

Martin Bradshaw, Director of the Civic Trust, warmly welcomed the report, hitting the nail on the head with his remarks. "A town centre needs a lot more than just shops to remain vital", said Bradshaw. "Since superstores are now part of our shopping pattern, we need to re-think the role of our centres, which means living as well as working - communality, culture and conviviality as well as commerce."

Recently, the British Government released a response to the House of Commons Committee report that almost wholly endorsed the committee's recommendations. In one of its strongest concessions, the Government agreed to revise an important statutory planning policy guideline, especially with regard to the location of new retailing schemes. Tests will be applied to new retail developments and car parking in town centres. The Secretary of State for the Environment also expressed his commitment to safeguarding the vitality of towns and the economic viability of their retail centres.

The Royal Town Planning Institute was quick to express delight over the Government's response and called for immediate action and a sustained commitment. "Any slide back to the free market free-for-all", said an Institute spokesperson, "would be disastrous".

Back in Canada, superstore sprawl proceeds apace. Ontario is the hotbed, but big boxes are popping up all over - Moncton recently approved it first (Cost-Co.). Provincial governments (responsible for planning policy in Canada) have generally been reluctant to step in to review the situation in a manner similar to the U.K. None has passed a law such as the State of Vermont. Ontario's Ministry of Municipal Affairs has shown some interest be commissioning a consultant's study titled, New Format Retailing and the Public Interest. Yet, there are some particularly worrying trends in existing regulatory practice. The Ontario Municipal Board (OMB), the administrative tribunal that sorts out local planning appeals, seems to be following a survival of the fittest approach, a kind of commercial Darwinism. It will not restrict large-format retailing because of the possible adverse effects on traditional stores. The Board's practice is to consider only two categories of impact that might warrant its intervention:

- blight caused by "over-storing that can lead to reduction in service or closure of stores in existing commercial centres, whether in a suburban location or historic core (literally, block-by-block decay), and

- threat to level of service enjoyed by the public as offered by existing and planned shopping facilities.

More problematic, according to one expert, is the recent tendency of the Board to shift the burden of proof from the proponent of the superstore development to the objectors, in determining whether or not adverse effects are likely to occur with respect to the two categories indicated above.

Amongst the few prominent Canadians that have voiced concern over the superstore, none is more perceptive and passionate that John Sewell, a former mayor

Back in Canada, superstore sprawl proceeds apace, Ontario is the hotbed, but big boxes are popping up all over - Moncton recently approved its first (CostCo). Provincial Governments (responsible for planning policy in Canada) have generally been reluctant to step in to review the situation in a manner similar to the U.K.

of Toronto. Many will recall that he recently served as Chariman of the Commission on Planning and development Reform in Ontario. In a speech to the 1994 Downtown Conference in Saint John, New Brunswick, Sewell sent out a clarion call, saying superstore sprawl threatened the very survival of our older downtowns.

Just as concerned activists and official in the U.S. and the U.K., John Sewell is not worried about big stores, but their location. He wants proposed superstores to be controlled by zoning in a way that makes them locate downtown. Sewell has in mind the former downtown "big" stores like Eaton's and Simpson's that created a retailing focal point around which smaller specialty stores thrived. Some have argued that because superstore need large sites, such developments downtown could only locate on abandoned industrial land and would still undermine inner-city main-street shopping, and add pressure for more roads aimed at the city centre.

Nevertheless, Sewell feels that key to the viability of superstore location downtown is recognition of the multi-purpose use of city centres. Sewell urges that this approach be strengthened by encouraging lots of housing around Main Street, utilizing residential properties for home-based businesses, and attracting cultural communities and new immigrants with their diverse and lively traditions. Equally important, Sewell says that a campaign needs to be launched to end subsidies for suburban development (especially infrastructure) and to break political alliances between municipal, provincial and federal governments that encourage the suburban style.

Sadly, except for sporadic newspaper coverage, John Sewell is a voice crying in the wilderness compared to the groundswell of public concern being expressed in America and Britain. Canadians are asleep at the switch on this critical urban conservation issue. It's time to wake up and turn it on!

Pathways to Sustainability

Igor Vojnovic

Igor Vojnovic is currently a Ph.D. candidate, teaching a graduate course in urban design at the University of Toronto. He is also a Research Associate with ICURR, the Intergovemmental Committee on Urban and Regional Research and is currently heading a project on municipal consolidation.

Appropriate Pricing Within Urban Economies

Modern cities are filled with irrational pricing mechanisms. This has been recognized since the 1960's when Thompson argued that "the price of using urban fringe space has been set too low — well below the full costs of running pipes, wires, police cars, and fire engines farther than would be necessary if building lots were smaller" (Thompson 1968, P.28). In fact, the existence of the modern city, characterized by high urbanization rates and rapid resource exploitation, seems to depend on the under-pricing of goods and services. This has been well documented within Africa and is usually referred to as the urban bias. During the 1960's price controls in African cities were established to contain urban inflation. Government intervention ensured under-priced urban services and agricultural products from the rural economy. Some African nations also maintained a fixed exchange rate above the market value, encouraging the import of cheaper and more preferred agricultural products. These factors promoted a continuous decline in the rural economy and rapidly accelerated urbanization (Stren and White 1989).

The under pricing of private and public goods and services within urban centers has also been recognized within the North American context, however, the implications of this condition have not been appropriately assessed. The under-pricing of urban commodities has not only encouraged rapid urbanization, but it has also developed metropolitan regions that are less efficient in their consumption of energy, material and land. The under-pricing of goods and services within urban centers, such as transportation and its required infrastructure, has encouraged a supra-optimal demand for these services, which in turn has resulted in an over-exploitation of resources. By encouraging urban centers to become more economically efficient — reflecting social costs in infrastructure, land, and energy — urban forms would have a propensity to intensify to a more compact pattern of development. The progression of cities to a more compact form would be generated by the increased costs of goods and services resulting from the new approaches in pricing. Therefore, the propensity towards higher densities would be driven strictly by market forces once the correct pricing initiatives are introduced. There are conceivable scenarios, however, under which this relationship would not hold. For instance, certain consumers, upper income earners specifically, may maintain a preference for housing in low density developments and be willing to pay for it. This means that increases in the price of urban goods may not necessarily encourage more compact developments in all markets. Nonetheless, on the whole, more compact developments would be encouraged by the new pricing initiatives.

Determining The Correct Pricing of Urban Goods and Services

In recognition that it is very difficult for the private market to determine the correct monetary value of all the urban goods and services, a number of economic tools can be introduced by the public sector to accommodate the proposed pricing initiatives. By imposing environmental charges, charges on particular human activities creating ecological problems, such as private automobile use, and user charges, levies on the use of collective goods and services, such as public infrastructure, communities can improve on current pricing practices. Deciding the optimal environmental charge that would lead to the appropriate pricing of private and public goods and services within

urban centers is extremely complex and expensive. However, ignoring the problem and allowing economic inefficiencies to persist while current environmental stresses intensify is a choice that should clearly be reassessed. The answer to this problem can, potentially, be found in the billing practice. User and environmental charges can be utilized to provide marginal increases, by politically acceptable amounts, in the price of public and private goods that are under-priced. Municipal governments can then monitor the effects of these price increases on the local market. If consumption patterns were improved with the initial price adjustments then a second round of price increases could be initiated, and so on. Realistically, an optimum price would be difficult to establish because of the market dynamics. However, this process would guarantee greater efficiency within urban regions, and in the overall use of resources, than currently exists.

Physical Flows Within Urban Regions And Their Costs

If municipalities are to encourage correct pricing within urban regions, an important consideration will be the assessment of physical flows. Cities commonly generate significant waste by-products that must be accounted for in physical flow evaluations of urban systems. For instance, pollutant emissions from transportation services within cities are physical flows that do have costs associated with them. Some of these costs are apparent in health care, impacts on acute respiratory diseases and cancer caused by volatile organic compounds, and in damage to wildlife and vegetation from sulfur oxide and nitrogen oxide emissions. However, urban systems do not account for these physical flows in the price of the car, gasoline, or road use.

A comprehensive understanding of the physical flows within cities would enable planners to make decisions that are more reflective of existing conditions — enabling greater precision in the pricing of urban commodities. Untreated wastewater discharge presents a classic example of potential problems associated with ignoring physical flows. Since the

"Taken together, the studies (on the cost of sprawl) reach similar conclusions: development spread out at low densities increases the costs of public facilities."

Source: Douglas R. Porter, in the foreward to *The Costs of Alternative Development Patterns*, by James E. Frank, 1989.

19th century, cities have concentrated great efforts at improving human health. Unfortunately, many of the advances came at the expense of environmental well-being. Because of the untreated waste-water discharge, the introduction of piped water and sewer systems to combat disease polluted bodies of water, air, and soil. Since the complete physical flows of human activities were not accounted for, the wastewater discharge created serious environmental aberrations but did not impose any immediately recognizable costs or losses. (Gordon 1990, P. 15) However, the environmental deterioration caused by these sanitation decisions ultimately limited the degree to which the quality of public health was improved. The costs of these decisions, evident in terms of both environmental and social harm, became apparent later.

Correct Pricing Initiatives: Water Provision And Private Automobile Use

Most municipalities in Canada do not recover water provision costs, or include the price of water itself in the charge. This is true even in regions that consider water a scarce resource. In fact, the very idea of charging for the water itself is unfamiliar. We need to recognize, however, that while water is never used up, after its use it is never returned to the environment in exactly the same form it was received. Also, during the time in which it is diverted to a given human use, it is not available for alternative uses. Municipal water charges in Canada also rarely cover the service costs of providing water to the consumers. Due to the under-pricing of water, there is little economic incentive to promote efficient consumption patterns of this resource. This results in over-consumption of water by both the residential and the commercial users. Furthermore, the Government of Canada contends "the revenue shortfall resulting from consumers paying less than the full cost of water services can discourage municipalities from undertaking investments in facilities to treat wastewater," thereby producing serious environmental and social harm with the raw discharge (Environment Canada 1992, P. 46).

France and Germany, on the other hand, are not only recovering the full costs of water provision, but have also introduced effluent charges to recover the external costs of municipal water use. On average, their price of providing 1,000 gallons of water is about $10, a price considerably higher than that in Canada. It is also roughly three times higher than the charge to a City of Toronto resident (City of Toronto 1990, Pp. 9-10). As expected, the under-pricing of water leads to an over-use. The average consumption per capita per day in Canadian municipalities averages to roughly 350 litres, while the average consumption per capita per day in both French and German cities is maintained at about 150 litres (City of Toronto 1990, Pp. 9-10).

There are also higher marginal costs associated with pumping water to low density suburbs of the Greater Toronto Area (GTA) than to the inner city. If appropriately evaluated, the "correct marginal-cost pricing of these urban services would result in higher rates being charged in these areas" (Bird and Slack 1983). Since marginal-cost pricing is not currently incorporated, there are no incentives for home buyers to reconsider their demand for spread developments. The problem is further compounded because developers are not levied an appropriate charge for the provision of infrastructure in new developments. Municipalities usually find the marginal cost pricing of hard infrastructure expensive, as it would have to be done on a site by site basis. As a result, most governments levy a uniform charge across their jurisdiction, which does not reflect the full cost of infrastructure, and encourages a supra-optimal demand. The under-pricing of infrastructure, therefore, invites non-contiguous developments and spread building configurations within subdivisions.

Perhaps the classic case of under pricing in North American cities is associated with the private automobile. It has been argued that if the social costs of automobile use were correctly evaluated, the price of the car, or gasoline per litre, would increase roughly nine-fold. For instance, Los Angeles subsidizes "55 per

Studies conducted over the last 30 years have concluded that when development is spread out at low densities, the per-unit cost of constructing and maintaining public facilities increases. The reason for this is that low-density development requires more miles of roads, curbs, sewers, and water lines; and municipal services must be delivered over a greater geographic area."

Source: The Land Institute, *The Case for Multifamily Housing*, 1991.

cent of the workforce driving to work daily ... between $56 to $74 million annually in free parking alone" (Fowler 1991). The under pricing of the private car in North America has resulted in its over-use. This is reflected in a per capita gasoline consumption in most U.S. and Canadian cities that is more than four times that of European cities, and over 10 times greater than Asian cities (Newman and Kenworthy 1989, P.25). While in Los Angeles, Denver, Detroit, and Houston, between 88 per cent and 94 per cent of the population drives to work, in Europe only 40 per cent of the urban residents drive, and in industrialized Asian cities, such as Tokyo, only 15 per cent of the citizens drive. In fact, the average US family spends more money on the car than on food, with average automobile and related expenditures accounting for 25 per cent of household income (Roseland 1992, p.107).

Similar patterns of automobile use are also apparent in Canada. It has been claimed that in the 1989-90 fiscal year the real social costs of automobile use were over eight billion dollars, all of which was subsidized by the Ontario government (Pollution Probe 1991, P.61). It has been argued that if a gasoline tax is used to recover the external costs of the private automobile the price of gasoline would increase to $5 per litre. The supra-optimal use of the private automobile resulting from under-pricing is well illustrated in the GTA. In 1986, out of 488,900 households in the outer suburbs, only one per cent were without an automobile, and 64 per cent of the households had two or more cars. (Gilbert 1991, p.5).

Extreme reliance on the private automobile has not only encouraged the spread of North American cities, but has also increased the levels of associated resource consumption and environmental degradation. In comparison, the lower dependence on the car in Europe is considered to be the critical variable that has continued to generate more compact developments, where the distances urban Europeans travel to work and on daily errands are 50 per cent shorter on average than similar trips in North America (Brown 1987, P.19). Encouraging correct pricing of private transportation would

generate an alternative use of available resources that would affect consumption patterns and development configurations. For instance, after the Federal Government in Ottawa increased the parking rates for its employees, there was a 23 per cent reduction in employees driving to work, a 16 per cent increase in transit ridership among federal employees, and an increase in average vehicle occupancy from 1.33 to 1.41 passengers (Roseland 1992, p.94).

The benefits that would accrue from the new consumption patterns would be realized at a number of different levels. First, the increase in the price of the car would encourage a shift to alternative modes of transportation, such as public transit, walking and cycling, thereby increasing levels of environmental preservation. A 1990 study by the Canadian Urban Transit Association has indicated that shifting just five per cent of the peak period car trips to transit in the GTA would result in savings of more than 150,000 trips and more than 1,570,000 vehicle kilometers per working day (Paehlke 1991, P.12-13). Examining the benefits of reduced emissions alone, 3.6 tonnes of volatile organic compounds (VOCs), 3.1 tonnes of nitrogen oxides (NOx), and 4,226 tonnes of carbon dioxides (CO2) would be eliminated each working day.

Second, the shift away from the car would also encourage more compact forms of development, in order to make public transit, walking and cycling more effective transportation alternatives. Without an affordable automobile, low density suburbs would no longer be feasible. Suburban developments might take on a form similar to that of the streetcar suburbs, such as Riverside or Forest Hills Gardens. Since the residents of these suburbs did not rely on the car for transportation, the developments were more compact, with densities roughly four times greater than the average current suburb in North America (Rybczynski 1991, p.72).

Benefits to the household would also be realized as the money saved on the private automobile would be available for alternative, and perhaps more socially beneficial uses — assuming that an

" streets, utilities, and schools for a suburban single family development with three dwelling units per acre built five miles from sewage and water treatment plants in a leapfrog pattern would cost $43,381 per dwelling in 1987 dollars. Building the same development adjacent to existing development and near central facilities would reduce the cost by $11,597 per dwelling unit, a 27 per cent reduction."

Source: Centre for Urban Studies (PSU) and Regional Financial Advisors, Inc. *DLCD's Local Government Infrastructure Funding in Oregon,* 1990.

This article is an excerpt from a report prepared for the **Centre for Urban & Community Studies** on sustainability.

attractive public transit system was made available. For a lower income household that does not own property, an increase in income of 25 per cent might make the purchase of a house more accessible, a wiser investment than the private automobile. In the U.S. the Institute for Transportation and the Environment notes that young families are often advised by banks to sell a second auto in order to qualify for a mortgage (Roseland 1992, p.107).

Conclusion

Advancement towards sustainability will be generated by encouraging an optimal allocation of resources. Encouraging economic efficiency would ensure that resource depletion by any one generation is minimized, while allowing the current generation to improve present standards of living through increased levels of productivity. A similar progression towards sustainability would be realized with urban forms. By recognizing true costs in the pricing of urban commodities, urban regions would intensify to a more compact and efficient pattern of development. This would inevitably reduce their consumption of energy, material, and land. Advancement towards sustainable urban forms, therefore, would be generated through increased efficiency in various functions within the city and by subsequent improvements in natural ecological preservation.

Rethinking Ownership

Russell Mawby

Russell Mawby was the founder and Director of the Collaborative Housing Society, which is implementing a number of initiatives to facilitate shared ownership as a viable tenure option. He is currently the Social Housing Facilitator for the City of Saskatoon.

Our cities and towns are shaped by many forces and circumstances, but one of the most important elements is also the most ignored. Attitudes and assumptions about how we own and trade property are usually overlooked in discussions about urban development, and yet they underlie most of our decisions about planning, building codes, construction and development practices, and even building form.

The effects of these attitudes are readily apparent in the fabric of our cities. Compare two of Toronto's older residential neighbourhoods, Cabbagetown and Parkdale. Both were considered slums in the late 1960's, with Cabbagetown, a dense sea of Victorian rowhouses, in the process of being erased and transformed into those bold experiments of social engineering, the point tower and the housing project. Parkdale was once the domain of the well-to-do, but by this time its luxurious mansions had long been broken up into rooms and apartments, with a few cleared away for smaller scale towers, a supermarket and other modern innovations.

Now, thirty years later, the remains of Cabbagetown have been gentrified into one of Toronto's more desirable downtown neighbourhoods, while Parkdale is still an enclave of rooming houses and cheap apartments, with a higher percentage of rental units than the average for the rest of Toronto. All other factors aside, the small, easily divisible row houses that make up most of Cabbagetown are easier for single households to own, and thus finance. Parkdale's mansions remain as rooming houses because we have no easy way for individuals to divide ownership of them, except as landlords.

Considering urban form as a map of our attitudes towards property is valuable for two reasons. First of all, changing our point of view is a powerful tool for highlighting issues and opportunities. The need for testing our assumptions is becoming acute as we start to understand that, rather than more social engineering and national housing programs, we need to cultivate local solutions that are rooted in the community. The term that best captures this is "enablement", as it considers development from the perspective of residents within a community. The real benefit of an enablement approach is that it mobilizes local resources, enabling supports and amenities that can greatly benefit the full range of individual and family needs beyond those of mere shelter.

Of equal importance, however, is that simply tinkering with new urban forms is becoming irrelevant in the face of a systemic failure of development mechanisms which we have taken for granted for so long. The disappearance of both government funding and the "traditional" homebuyer are each raising new considerations (and opportunities) for development that prevailing ownership mechanisms do not seem to take into account.

Households are no longer necessarily made up of nuclear families, if they ever were. We are beginning to demand more from our housing than mere shelter, as ideas about living and working at or near home take root. Social services are increasingly being located in the home and neighbourhood, yet much of our housing stock seems ill-suited to supporting anything other than a two-parent, car-driving family. Throw in concepts like intensification and mainstreets, and we have a rich variety of housing needs poorly served by a limited palette of housing options.

Our deficiency of options becomes acutely apparent when we look at what is happening elsewhere in the world. London's flats or New York's co-ops, not to mention the over 120 groups across North America actively pursuing collaborative enablement approaches via co-housing. But even here in Canada there are many inventive approaches to housing that we can learn from. For example, British Columbia and Alberta's Strata Title legislation is assumed to be equivalent to Ontario's Condominium Act, and yet there are some interesting and inventive housing developments going on out West that would be difficult if not impossible to implement in Ontario - equity co-ops on leased land being just one example. Does Ontario's Condominium Act limit ownership options, or is it just that our attitudes and assumptions cause us to overlook alternatives and innovations? Either way, there seems to be a much broader range of housing opportunities than convention would suggest.

Consider the following: Statistics Canada recently reported that 40 per cent of single people in Canada now own their own homes. What they didn't report is that an increasing number of those homeowners are actually sharing the ownership of their homes. Primarily a phenomenon of downtown neighbourhoods, housing partnerships offer a positive choice for many people, especially in this age of downsizing and empty nesters. It offers a desirable alternative to renting, an affordable option for downtown living, and a way of using existing housing stock to acceptably maintain and intensify our downtown neighbourhoods. Sharing also presents other advantages, not the least of which is companionship and security, but also the opportunity to share other amenities such as laundry facilities, photocopiers and fax machines, gardening equipment, and in some cases, cars.

Of course, sharing housing already occurs in the form of rental apartments. Renting is an important tenure option and will always be a necessary, even though it may sometimes be an inadequate housing choice. Yet given the benefits conferred by home ownership, and the corresponding low-esteem renting holds in the general scheme of things, it cannot be the only mechanism available for adaptive re-use of existing housing, especially if, with the threatened repeal of Bill 120, accessory apartments become illegal once again.

Yet, however appealing shared ownership may be for some people, it remains a difficult solution. The problem isn't in setting up a partnership; it's at the other end of the transaction that the difficulties lie, particularly when only one partner wishes to move on. Even if a new partner is ready, willing and able to take over the departing share, just try to get mortgage financing on half a house. As a consequence, most partnerships end up dissolving, sometimes acrimoniously.

The difficulties are only magnified when we consider community-based ownership-sharing on a larger scale. Equity co-ops or co-ownerships have a chequered past, but there are occasions when the common resource embodied in a housing development should remain in the common realm. This is the basis for

...housing partnerships offer a positive choice for many people, especially in this age of downsizing and empty nesters. It offers a desirable alternative to renting, an affordable option for downtown living, and a way of using existing housing stock to acceptably maintain and intensify our downtown neighbourhoods.

the Toronto Islands Land Trust, which could have provided access to individual financing under the umbrella of community-based control over land use. This would ensure long-term affordability and security of tenure, while preserving the unique development patterns that make the community what it is. Political and other considerations are muddying the waters of this potentially powerful new way of enabling community, but so is the unwillingness of lenders to extend mortgages, partly because the expected boundaries of ownership are murkier than banks would like. A straight-forward condominium-type tenure with some mechanism to preserve affordability might have solved the problem without resorting to complex and convoluted legislation.

Consider also one of those 120 collaborative housing projects in the works throughout North America, where perhaps five years of effort will have gone into creating a place that not only provides affordable units, but could also provide a shared work center, with photocopier and fax machine, room to hold meetings, and other supports for work-at-home. There is a strong incentive to preserve the common good of affordability, as well as to encourage a commitment and responsibility to the other common resources, and yet every conventional development and ownership mechanism we use tends to shift control to the individual and dilute responsibility to the community.

It could well be argued that it is our attitudes towards property, reinforced by our tenure forms, that have destroyed the ability of our communities to work together. Some form of mutual responsibility and ownership is required to make these systems work.

But in the end, rethinking our assumptions about property and ownership is not so much about introducing fancy new alternatives to the housing scene as it is about enabling people to find or make their own solutions, making their housing adapt to their needs rather than vice versa. It is important to understand that ownership mechanisms are not so much a cause of our housing problems, as they are a symptom of systemic attitudes about the role housing plays in our society. If we are serious about finding new ways of building and living in our cities and towns, we can no longer ignore these attitudes that are at the heart of why we build.

Density and Urban Form: Sorting Out the Confusions

John Hitchcock

A number of measures are commonly employed to measure urban density in discussions about urban intensification, reflecting varying choices for both numerator and denominator. More often than not, these discussions fail to indicate which particular measure is intended. To complicate things further, there is no consensus in the use of terms, so that even when a measure is identified, one still may not be entirely sure what was meant. Let us review four measures, proceeding from the smallest to the most inclusive denominator, using a numerical example to indicate the effect that choice of measure has on the numerical density value. To keep the illustration simple, the same numerator (number of residential units)

John Hitchcock, until his recent retirement, was a Professor of Geography at the University of Toronto

will be maintained throughout. I have assigned a name to each measure which is intended to be self explanatory. Alternative terms in use are included in parentheses. Following this description, some related sources of confusion will be briefly discussed.

Measures of Density

Parcel Density (net net density, net site density, net density, lot density). In this measure the denominator is the sum of all individual parcels of land (or lots) on which residential units are built. Parcel density is the least ambiguous density measure in the sense that the denominator, whether it is a single parcel or an aggregation of separate parcels, has a precise definition, and the area(s) involved are normally carefully measured and contained in a legal record of some sort.

To provide a numerical example, let us assume the town of Utopia is a total of 8 hectares in size. It has one residential neighbourhood which contains 32 single family units, each located on a private parcel of land with an area of 625 square metres. (This is roughly equivalent to lots 60 feet wide by 110 feet deep). The aggregate area occupied by these 32 parcels is 20,000 square metres, or 2 hectares. The parcel density of Utopia's neighbourhood then is 32 units per 2 hectares, or 16 units per hectare. (This is roughly equivalent to 6.5 units per acre.) Note that Utopia's statistics are obviously simplified for illustrative purposes, but they are consistent with some very rough rules of thumb about land use.

Street Density (net density). This measure increases the land base over which density is calculated by adding the area of public street rights-of-way (i.e., the street plus sidewalk, if any, plus any additional area needed for underground services, etc.) needed to gain access to the parcel. This alternative measure is useful for comparing an area which has already been developed with public streets to an area which is undeveloped, or which has been developed with private streets, as might be the case with a condominium townhouse project. The denominator for this density measure is normally taken to be the total area of parcels plus one half of the public rights-of-way which abut the parcels (i.e., typically the right-of-way is shared by two lots). Since rights-of-way may vary from one place to another, and corner lots and arterial streets may be treated a number of ways, street densities are only roughly comparable. In Utopia, street rights-of-way constitute 25 per cent of its total land area (including residential and non-residential areas). Since Utopia's residential neighbourhood includes uses other than houses (to be considered in moment), we will assume that the street area abutting our 32 residential parcels totals .667 hectare. (In southern Ontario street rights-of-way are commonly 66 feet.

Half of this would be 33 feet or roughly one third the length of a 110 foot lot.) In Utopia, street density is 32 units /[2 hectares + .667 hectares], or 12 units per hectare.

Gross Residential Area Density (gross site density, residential density, residential area density, gross density, living area density, neighbourhood density). This density measure is frequently used because many residential areas contain a relatively limited range of non-residential uses, such as parks, schools, churches, libraries, community centres and so on. It can be used to estimate the amount of land needed for a new subdivision of X units, taking into account these residentially related uses. In Utopia's residential neighbourhood of 32 units, the parcels on which residentially related uses are located take up 1 hectare, and the rights-of-way which provide access to them take up another .333 hectares. Its residential areas (residential parcels, rights-of-way, and residentially related uses), therefore, occupy 50 per cent of the total land area of the municipality. Its Gross Residential Area (GRA) density is 32 units /[2 hectares + .667 hectare + one hectare + .333 hectare], or eight units per hectare.

Gross Municipal Area Density (gross density, community density). In Utopia all of the land has been developed for urban purposes. (In our accounting, park land is an urban use even though it is not built up.) Fifty per cent of its land area is devoted to its residential neighbourhood, as described above, and the remaining 50 per cent is devoted to commercial and industrial land, regional parks, and public rights-of-way. Its gross municipal area density, therefore, is 32/8 hectares, or four units per hectare. Note that if Utopia contained land which was currently vacant but intended for urban development, its gross municipal area density would be lower, but would not be strictly comparable to the density of another municipality which was completely developed.

In discussing density in relation to intensification, then, it is obviously important to know which measure is being used.

It is not uncommon .. for tall apartment buildings in suburban settings ... to be developed at lower densities than much lower buildings in the central area ... with less land around them, even though one's visual impression might reverse this ranking.

Relation to Urban Form

Any density measure is an imperfect indicator of the kind of development which can occur at any particular place. A given density can be achieved in many ways; a density figure, by itself, does not indicate the nature of the urban form which generates that particular density. A very wise planner from Toronto named Hans Blumenfeld wrote an article some years ago comparing Metropolitan Toronto with Hamburg. The interesting point was that, at the time the article was written, the two municipalities had very similar gross municipal densities, but as urban environments they were completely different. The differences are complex and do not permit easy summarization here. But in very general terms, Hamburg's residential areas comprised single-family dwellings in the form of rowhouses and apartments in medium-rise structures, while Metro Toronto's residential areas were marked by single-detached houses at low density and tall apartment buildings at a much higher density.

It is perhaps useful to think of density as an average. On one or two lots the density in any one place will necessarily be close to the average, but as the land base of the denominator increases, the given density figure tells us less and less about how spot densities on particular sites will vary from the average. Even if we know the spot density for a particular site, however, we still won't know what the built form will be like. Structures might be short and fat, or tall and skinny. It is not uncommon, for example, for tall apartment buildings in suburban settings around Toronto to be developed at lower densities than much lower buildings in the central area which are developed with less land around them, even though one's visual impression might reverse this ranking. At the least inclusive end of the scale, parcel density, a given density measure tells us nothing about the allocation of land to various uses outside the individual residential parcels. Small lots, for example, might abut large rights-of-way or be located in residential areas with large parks.

Depending on their particular

> ... there should be a requirement that urban form be explicitly described rather than murkily alluded to by a density figure.

experience, people tend to associate a given density with one particular urban form. In fact, density tells us relatively little about urban form. If a debate about intensification is concerned with the desirability or undesirability of a particular urban form, there should be a requirement that the urban form be explicitly described rather than murkily alluded to by a density figure.

Land Consumption

Our imaginary city of Utopia can serve to illustrate another source of confusion. Because the measures which planners frequently use are residential densities, it is not surprising that exhortations to intensify typically assume that the only way to do this is to increase parcel or street densities. Let us revisit land use in Utopia to illustrate why this is misleading.

Residential parcels make up only 25 per cent of the land area of Utopia. Even if we double Utopia's parcel density, we will lower Utopia's total land consumption from eight to seven hectares, or a reduction of 12.5 per cent. If the objective of intensification is to reduce the total amount of land being consumed for urban purposes, then public policy needs to consider ways to reduce the land consumption of all uses, not just residential ones. While Utopia very roughly reflects the order of magnitude of various major land uses, we do not know to any degree of accuracy how much of the land in our cities is being used for what purposes. We might suspect, however, that automobile related uses consume a great deal of land. We not only provide roads for the automobile, but we are increasingly providing parking for it at any of the destinations it might conceivably want to head for. Large new suburban shopping complexes duplicate existing commercial floor space and consume much additional land for parking. New low density manufacturing plants and automated warehouses represent other kinds of uses which contribute to the overall total of land consumed for urban purposes, and so forth. If we wish to reduce total land consumption in any significant way, then we need to seriously consider the way we build all parts of our cities, not just their residential units.

Density and Quality of Life

Suburbia on the Edge

Lois E. Nesbitt

Ask residents of West Windsor where the township's downtown is, and chances are they'll mention a gauntlet of shopping plazas and strip malls divided by Route 71. West Windsor, like many New Jersey townships, was transformed during the 1980s economic boom from an older community surrounded by farmland into just one piece of a sprawling suburban landscape, a mesh of old towns, new subdivisions, major retail centers, and corporate headquarters.

These new conglomerations - dubbed "edge cities" - began to appear at the end of the boom decade, conveying a vision shared by developers, corporations, retailers, and homeowners that America's golden future was a place where people could live, work, and shop without having to trundle to an old-fashioned downtown or make a long commute to a distant city. Utopia, in edge city, is measured in leaseable square feet, ten-minute drives to the office, and three-bedroom colonials with two-car garages.

But edge cities began to spread across the landscape, eating up all the open space in their way, and now this vision of utopia has begun to lose its glow. High-speed roads blaze through neighborhoods. Shopping compounds produce all-day bottlenecks. Condos sprout where farms once stood, then stand empty, unsold. And hanging heavy over the suburban sprawl is the sense that, as Gertrude Stein put it, "There's no there there." Many residents of West Windsor (the edge city that it's now part of goes by the graceless moniker "the Princeton-to-New Brunswick Route 1 Corridor") complain that they miss a sense of identity, of place. It's telling how many of the township's subdivisions carry the name of the only significant old town nearby: Prince-

ton Oaks, Princeton Chase, Princeton View, Princeton Greens.

Edge cities have spread out not only along Mercer County's Route 1 corridor but in other parts of New Jersey as well. The Meadowlands/Hoboken area in Bergen County; the region surrounding the Bridgewater Mall, comprising parts of Somerset, Union, and Hunterdon counties; and the Woodbridge and Metropark areas of Middlesex County are all examples of the phenomenon.

Robert Fisherman, professor of history at Rutgers-Camden and author of *Bourgeois Utopias: The Rise and Fall of Suburbia,* sees edge cities as the third phase in recent suburban history. First came the postwar housing boom, which the Federal Housing Association promoted through a national highway system and mortgage insurance policies that favored single-family homes. Then came the stores: strip shopping centers in the 1960s, followed by the "malling of America" in the 1970s. Finally, cheap real estate in the 1980s encouraged savvy corporations to move their headquarters out of cities and into the "edge."

"Eighty per cent of all rental office space built in the 1980s went up in edge cities," says James Hughes, professor of urban planning and policy development and associate dean of Rutgers' Edward J. Bloustein School of Planning and Public Policy. "For New Jersey, this meant an increase of 622,000 jobs between 1982 and 1987." But that was the boom. Since 1989, says Hughes, the state has lost 200,000 jobs in corporate downsizings. Office buildings stand empty while high-end shops give way to discount outlets that cater to, as Hughes says, "Aging, disappointed yuppies who want quality but don't want to pay for it."

Lois E. Nesbitt is a freelance writer living in New York City.

This article was republished, with permission, from Rutgers Magazine, Winter 1993.

Housing permits throughout the state bottomed out in 1991 at 14,700, and developers learned to think small.

A Virginia-based monthly newsletter, Edge City News, calls the 1990s the "re-decade: It's time to renew, rethink, remake, revive, rebuild, revitalize, reinvest, restructure, recycle, reposition, retrench, remodel, retrofit, resize, resell, and retire but never retreat." Rutgers' Fishman agrees: "Every new urban scheme goes through this confusion, with inappropriate models and overbuilding." He calls for a broad reconsideration of what the edge city is all about and cites two priorities for New Jersey in the 1990s: (1) to save some open space from the bulldozers, and (2) to rethink every aspect of the suburban environment.

Anton Nelessen, professor of urban planning and policy development at Rutgers, thinks some solutions to edge-city anomie lie in the past. In research conducted across the country, Nelessen says he sees a nostalgia for two-lane Main Streets and colonial landscapes that indicates Americans don't like the communities they've created.

Twelve years ago, at Rutgers, Nelessen developed Visual Preference Surveys, a way to gauge the likes and dislikes of residents seeking to redesign their communities. In places as far away as Portland, Oregon, and as close as Metuchen, New Jersey, Nelessen has presented to community groups a slide show of 240 pictures depicting a variety of American landscapes and architecture. The audience is asked to rate each slide on a scale of minus 10 to plus 10. Invariably, people given high marks to New England villages, farmsteads, and traditional Main Street U.S.A. communities. The lowest marks go to strip malls, state highways, and suburban tract housing.

"Across the board, people reject suburban sprawl and view small communities as positive," says Nelessen. "What we've created for ourselves is not the place where we'd live if we had the choice." John and Jane Q. Public like trees; they like Boston's Back Bay with its fabric of four- and five-storey brick row houses;

they like communities with "visual termination," planning jargon for the sense of enclosure intimated by public squares and narrow, grid-pattern streets.

But how can Americans' nostalgia for old-time town life mesh with a landscape governed by the automobile and the suburban mansion? Nelessen declares that the American family, already "taxed to the max by the cost of cars, of pollution" and what he perceives as the "social disintegration of the family that never eats together anymore," would rather have fewer cars and a smaller house.

A proponent of neotraditional planning, Nelessen envisions hybrid towns in which "new technologies, new materials, and new life-styles are laid over historic models." Nelessen believes that what he calls "the pedestrian realm" is the key to creating communities with a sense of place. "People prefer a more traditional setting where they can get to know their neighbors and walk to the corner store to buy a quart of milk; where there is a bona fide downtown with small shops, personalized services, a post office, library, churches, and other community institutions," he says. "This explains precisely why classic towns and villages - Princeton, New Jersey; New Hope, Pennsylvania; Annapolis, Maryland - remain so popular as places to live and visit."

Zoning regulations that mandate the separation of housing, jobs, and shopping have helped fuel the car culture and suburban sprawl. Nelessen sees mixed-use zoning (homes, stores, and offices on the same block or in the same building), pedestrian walkways, and narrow, slow-speed streets as central ingredients in recreating the community feel of pre-World War II town life. Some of the best news is that it's not too late to turn existing developments into what Nelessen calls "more humanistic 'communities of place'."

In Somerset County's Warren Township, for example, Nelessen developed a master plan to restrict and retain a small-town feel in the growing community. A key component was a design plan for the town's center to transform "inhuman parking lots into civilized streets that the

Nelessen's research reveals a nostalgia for some elements of old-time life: narrow streets, pedestrian walkways, downtown with shops and services.

community will be proud of." As part of the plan, village-style, mixed-use zoning regulations were drawn up. Strip malls were tied together with a looping road to serve as a Main Street, and the space between the malls was filled in with mixed-use buildings and pedestrian walkways that encouraged residents to stroll about.

Using the community's reaction to the Visual Preference Survey as a guideline for "a vision of what the people think the future can be," Nelessen has drawn up retrofitting plans for dozens of American communities, including the downtown's of five state capitals: Carson City, Nevada; St. Paul, Minnesota; Santa Fe, New Mexico; Little Rock, Arkansas; and Olympia, Washington. In New Jersey, Nelessen has redesigned areas of Highland Park, Berkeley Heights, and Pittstown, among others. "What we're about, more than anything else, is developing neighborhoods in the true sense of the word," says Nelessen.

His vision of retrofitting edge cities by encouraging the growth of village-like "nodes," as in the Warren Township design, is embraced by the New Jersey State Development and Redevelopment Plan. Adopted in 1987, the plan advocates managing growth by restricting new building to existing developed areas along roadways so that large tracts of open land can be saved from sprawl. This approach, if reality follows concept, will turn edge cities into "multivillages" of several connecting nodes. West Windsor's mayor, Tom Frascella, sees this concept as the only way to put a "there" into West Windsor: No one place in the township, he ways, is suited to become a genuine town center.

The New Jersey Plan, admirable as it is, has only advisory power and is already meeting resistance from local governments, says Diane Brake, chair of the Middlesex-Sommerset-Mercer Regional Council, a nonprofit organization that advises on development in the West Windsor area. But other forced checks on growth are coming from as high as the federal level and will have to be reckoned with: To conform with the federal Intermodal Surface Transportation Efficiency Act (ISTEA), New Jersey will have to cut commuting by 30 per cent or lose significant federal funding. And the Clean Air Act stipulates that companies with more than 100 employees must increase car occupancy among their commuters or the state will lose highway funding. These federal regulations provide yet another impetus for rethinking the juggernaut that is edge city.

Historically, the American response to an unsatisfactory situation is to strike out for new frontiers; any modern-day pioneering, however, will have to come in the form of applying innovations, like Nelessen's, to existing conditions. Unlike Huck Finn, we no longer have the option of moving on to the next unspoiled frontier across the next cornfield.

Partners in Crime

Lance Naismith

Intensification promotes an urban form which contradicts the planning and development norms of the past few decades. Intensification is seen as a possible means to reduce infrastructure costs and promote compact urban centres, thus aiding with the preservation of valuable greenland space surrounding the GTA and promoting greater transit oriented communities. Planners have the enviable position of helping to shape future urban structure; however, time lags involved in the adoption and implementation of plans may mean this is an ongoing and evolving process. Similarly, although police officers deal with existing communities, they also must respond to problems which develop over time.

Lance Naismith is a Staff Sergeant with the Metropolitan Toronto Police Force, Corporate Planning Unit. He has an educational background in Urban Planning at Sheridan College and in Criminology at the University of Toronto.

This article discusses the potential impacts that the built form can have on neighbourhood safety and, through a holistic viewpoint, promotes the need for planners, police, other professionals, and the public to work together to ensure that the future urban design encourages safe and secure communities.

Community input is encouraged during the planning process for development plan proposals requiring zoning amendments. The Not In My Backyard (NIMBY) syndrome is one sentiment often expressed during the planning process that can have significant effect on the development process. One concern often raised at public meetings, particularly for developments proposing higher densities, is that increased densities will also increase the probability of crime. This is a valid concern which can turn a public meeting into an emotional event for all parties involved. Moreover, upon observation of some planned urban areas, these concerns are very real. Ultimately, the issue of intensification creates a situation that involves an ongoing battle between community desires and the expectations of new developments. The pertinent question to be addressed by this article is: Does increasing population density cause the problem, or is it the way developments are planned?

Studies have illustrated that urban development impacts not only the built and natural environments, but also the social environment of a community. Therefore, it is imperative that future development applications and designs be sensitively planned to address the possible impacts of future development on the safety and security of residents. Although planners attempt to manage people and their environment, the emphasis on safety has been very limited and needs to be properly addressed. Traditionally, under the Planning Act of Ontario, concern for safety has been focused on traffic safety, rather than on resident safety. Safety of residents through potential changes in their environment must be examined, since changes to the urban form or structure may have an impact on the social and cultural conditions of the community.

This article is based on a presentation given at the OPPI Conference held in Niagra Falls, October 24th, 1993, moderated by Mr. Tom Smart of Miller O'Dell Associates.

In order to create optimal community designs, planners must begin to take a holistic view of planning, which should strive to ensure the safety of both present and future residents. The old adage, an ounce of prevention is worth a pound of cure, is quite appropriate in considering the social and financial costs that poor planning may impart on the existing community. Good urban design can and has had noticeable effects on the social development and well being of urban areas. Furthermore, since impacts of changes to a community become evident as the community matures over time, planners should be concerned with both the immediate and future ramifications that developments or changes may create on the community.

Crime And Urban Design

Does the built urban form, particularly in areas of greater densities, effect the safety of a community? Many studies have shown that a relationship between criminality and the urban form does exist. Although the type of crime and urban form may vary, there are four key requisites for a crime to occur. These include, the offender, the victim, the desire, and the opportunity to commit the crime.

Historically, criminals were deterred from committing crimes since they were usually the "new face in town" and were often forced away by the existing community. However, as the population of communities increases and become more transient, there are a greater number of strangers in our communities. As a society, we can no longer easily identify and force unwanted visitors or potential offenders from our communities. Therefore, in order to decrease crime rates or deter potential offenders, we must deal with one of the requisites of crime the opportunity element.

Design considerations which increase the visibility of a site may deter crime by making it difficult for an offender to strike without being witnessed. Hence, if the opportunity to commit a crime is less than ideal, crime may occur less frequently or not at all. Psychologist Harold M.

A Practitioner's Guide to Urban Intensification 43

Proshansky's study, Environmental Psychology: Man and His Physical Setting (1970), supports this claim and illustrates that an individual's physical surroundings will have an influence on his or her behaviour. According to Proshansky, if the physical setting is not conducive to a particular pattern of behaviour, this behaviour will be displaced to another, more vulnerable area. Exemplifying this, a study completed in 1991 by Professor Simon Hakim and Associate Professor Andrew Buck from Temple University in Philadelphia found that there is a greater risk of a break and enter into a residential dwelling if:

- the house is within three blocks of a major thoroughfare

- the house is on a cul-de-sac

- the house is adjacent to a wooded area, abandoned railroad tracks or a park

- the house is more expensive than others in the neighbourhood, and

- the occupants are relatively new to the area (within past year).

This research also found that break and enters into commercial premises generally occur in secluded sites where the chance of a crime being witnessed is less, providing criminals with more time to break into harder targets. Commonly, new firms, especially affluent looking firms were considered better targets. Notwithstanding the type of the unit, in both the residential and commercial cases, location was the prime factor inhibiting or enhancing crime. Another dominate factor identified in relation to crime in residential areas was short residency. Communities with a greater number of transient residents take less note of strangers.

Other Urban Factors

Levels of crime cannot solely be attributed to population density. There are other factors which must be closely examined and also taken into consideration.

First, areas of low residential population can suffer from higher crime rates due to factors such as the influx of tran-

sient populations (e.g., business or theatre districts). Secondly, in assessing levels of crime as related to density it is important to consider the crime rate in relation to population levels. The incidence of crime may be higher in areas with greater density, but crime per capita (crime rate) may be lower or the same as areas with lower densities. Thirdly, the way we design apartment buildings and housing units also has an influence on levels of crime. For example, the New York City Housing Authority has over the years retained detailed records illustrating that the grounds, lobbies, elevators, and stairs of apartments are areas prone to relatively high crime rates. The larger the apartment building, the more dangerous are these areas. Particularly dangerous spots are parking lots, enclosed areas that are not visible from the street or sidewalk, and laundry rooms. Similar conditions existed in the Pruitt-Igoe housing project in St. Louis that was demolished in the early 1980s (ten years after it was built) due to vandalism and high crime rates. In this case, there was a lack of defensible space, lack of social interaction, and lack of social control networks. These factors, coupled with the buildings' poor design and isolation of stairways, elevators, lobbies and hallways, created an almost natural environment for crime.

Ongoing studies commissioned by the Home Office in Great Britain take a somewhat different approach to crime and incorporate a number of demographic factors when making decisions on police deployment. One such factor is the "deprivation index" that is based on three components: the number of single parent families; the degree of overcrowding (number of people per room); and, unemployment rates in specific areas. They found that the higher the deprivation index, the greater the demand for police services and therefore an increased need for police resources in the area.

On the other hand, the study, Building Cities that Work (1992), completed by E.P. Fowler of York University determines that greater social and physical diversity in neighbourhoods can deter crime by promoting: more neighbour contact; lower

... the way we design apartment buildings and housing units also has an influence on levels of crime.

rates of juvenile delinquency; and, fewer incidents reported by residents. Common features of areas with these characteristics include a mixture of land uses and an interwoven park system. In addition, areas of high density and of mixed land uses also exhibit the positive factors that reflect lower crime rates, and thus a higher sense of safety among residents.

In sum, it can be seen that although similar attributes produce both positive and negative impacts on crime rates, the requisite of opportunity still remains dominant.

Finally, victimization studies confirm that opportunity is the most significant factor involved in many types of crime:

- By far, the greatest proportion of street crime and burglary is the result of opportunity, rather than of careful and professional planning by offenders. (Law Enforcement Assistance Administration Newsletter, Vol. 4, No. 3, 1974)

- "Areas of high crime density typically are both easily accessible to and well known by the criminal, are known to offer high likelihood of finding a victim at a given time and involve little risk of police apprehension." (Angel, S., Discouraging Crime through City Planning, 1968)

Offenders do not tend to be very mobile, and can be very territorial. Pro-active policing may cause criminals to re-establish themselves from one area to another. Therefore, without the proper support, one agency cannot effectively combat crime, and utilizing one tool alone will only make efforts ineffective.

These studies, illustrating factors affecting crime patterns, suggest that greater care must be taken in the design of areas that are zoned at higher densities. Land use planners must ensure that a broader, more involved evaluation of development plans are undertaken so as to ensure all socio-economic factors are considered prior to development. This holistic view of planning, including community input in symbiotic relationship

... urban areas must be designed to increase opportunities for residents to monitor their own neighbourhood.

with social planners, should increase the vitality of an urban area and decrease the potential for criminal activity. Ultimately, without proper consideration of the impact designs will have on the existing communities, the creation of urban crime ghettos will continue.

Crime Prevention Through Environmental Design

Police officers have traditionally been reactive to the problems faced when policing their community. This is the crime-fighting response. Over the last few years, however, police forces have begun to be more pro-active in their policing style, as emphasized with new inroads developing from Community Based Policing. One element that has been valued since the profession of policing began, is the value of community contributions and interaction with the police. Without the assistance of the community, police forces would be relatively ineffective in policing communities. Therefore, urban areas must be designed to increase opportunities for residents to monitor their own neighbourhood, and therefore decrease crime rates within those areas. This is especially true for areas of increased densities. Such initiatives have already begun within Canada and the United States. For example, police forces are working together with other social agencies to respond appropriately to safety and security issues, and to review the public safety implications of public works initiatives and major development proposals.

To initiate tasks effectively, all parties should follow appropriate guidelines that embrace the concepts of Crowe in "Environmental Security or Crime Prevention Through Environmental Design" in the National Prevention Institute (1991). This is an urban planning and design process that integrates crime prevention with neighbourhood design and urban development.

Ultimately, "the neighbourhood environment is dynamic and ever-changing. Over dependence on any one tool, whether law enforcement, social or physical structure, will not only fail but will ultimately diminish the effectiveness of the tool being used. A specific objective of Environmental Security is to provide a physical structure where the individual will be given opportunity, encouragement, and the means to extend the use and sphere of responsibility for (their) neighbourhood beyond the front door." (Gardiner, 1978,1) Through the analysis of future urban developments, the police and urban planners can become partners in inventing the means to ensure future citizen safety.

Conclusion

As our society and urban forms become more complicated, it is imperative that urban issues are studied from a multi-disciplinary perspective. This approach does not only apply to new developments. As our cities age, re-development or urban renewal will become much more important, giving us the opportunity to improve on past designs.

Planning documents should address the safety needs of the community in terms of social, urban and physical environments. While it is important that we consider the needs of the physical environment, we must also remember that any urban growth or development will impact on the human element for decades. Therefore, it is imperative that urban development is analyzed in conjunction with the publics' future safety in an organized and professional manner.

Some liaisons between local planners and neighbourhood police officers have already been developed. This should be encouraged to a greater degree, and should not be viewed as another stumbling block in the process. If this is accomplished, it can serve the dual need of obtaining public, as well as professional input, since neighbourhood officers will receive information regarding public concerns on a daily basis. Planning professionals, both public and private, should also continue to examine the effects that urban development will have on the surrounding communities (crime being one aspect) and, working with the policing community, design an urban form that will minimize criminal opportunities. If this sharing of knowledge and resources occurs, then we will indeed have Partners in Crime Prevention that benefits all communities involved.

On Intensification and Women-Friendly Cities

Kim England

Since the late 1980s discussions of intensification, reurbanization, redevelopment of Main Streets, reintegrating living and workplaces, and mixed land-use have peppered debates on urban from. Finally, geographers, planners, developers, and politicians are catching on to the advantages of designing women-friendly cities.

Segregated Cities: Not Just a Land-Use Issue

Feminists have argued for twenty years that cities with separated commercial, industrial and residential areas reflect ideas about the separation of public life (paid employment and political activity) and private life (home and family).

Public life has traditionally been associated with men and private sphere with women, so cities based on the segregation of land-uses are also cities based on segregated roles for women and men. Perhaps segregated cities worked better when most men were full-time workers and many women were full-time homemakers, but as women combine paid work with their domestic role they find themselves restricted by cities planned and built in the 1950s and 1960s around the assumption that women are full-time homemakers.

There is a finite period of time in each day into which various activities must be squeezed. Numerous studies, includ-

Kim England is an Assistant Professor of Geography at Scarborough College, University of Toronto

ing some as recently as 1994, indicate that married women in paid employment continue to do most of the domestic chores and child-care with little assistance from their husbands, who often only do the same amount of domestic work as men in "traditional" families. Cities designed around the spatial and functional separation of land uses are particularly difficult to negotiate when someone is simultaneously a parent (the child-care centre is in one place) and an employee (work is in another place) as well as having primary responsibility for managing the home (dry-cleaning and groceries have to be picked up at yet a third location which may be some distance from where you live). Of course, the complexity and stress of this intricate choreography is somewhat alleviated if you have a car (indeed, this choreography may only be possible if you do have a car because child-care and workplaces are otherwise inaccessible). The vast majority of adults in Toronto (and elsewhere) who do not have access to a car are women. Unfortunately, public transit is often not flexible enough to enable women to coordinate their daily activities, for example service is concentrated around "peak hours". In Toronto, this is complicated by a transportation system that is both focused on the downtown core and has a rectangular system of routes that requires time-consuming transfers for anyone moving diagonally across suburbs.

> Cities designed around the spatial and functional separation of land uses are particularily difficult to negotiate when someone is simultaneously a parent and an employee.

In Praise of Intensification

I see intensification as providing women, especially lone mothers, with opportunities to construct more flexible lives and enabling them to better facilitate their daily routines. Given the current attention being paid to the shifting structure and definition of the family, dual income couples (with or without children), parents with shared custody, lone parent, and blended families could all benefit from intensification. However, for intensification to "work" it must involve more than just residential intensification or increased densities. There needs to be a greater concentration and variety of activities (shops, restaurants, parks, child-care, schools, offices, community facilities, etc.).

Multi-purpose, mixed-use, compact neighbourhoods mean greater proximity to services (decreasing your reliance on a car), while higher densities provide sufficient concentrations of users to support a greater diversity and, therefore, choice of services within a smaller geographic area. At the same time, the fine grained morphology of high and medium density neighbourhoods can make it easier for women to develop locally-based social support systems and to share domestic responsibilities such as child-care. In fact, a number of studies in Canada and the US (including one conducted in Regent Park) indicate that some women in high-density urban neighbourhoods labeled as "uncoordinated," "disorganized" and "declining" by planners, find them desirable because they provide localized social support, paid jobs, child care and services. (This is interesting because neighbourhoods such as Regent Park do have the benefit of numerous localized activities, but do not have the right "form" of intensification, unlike, for example, St. Lawrence.)

Intensification might even aid the renegotiation of the division of labour between heterosexual couples. For example, commutes have lengthened over time, but men still travel further than women, which decreases the amount of time that they can spend with their families. Intensification would allow men (and women) to spend less time commuting, and at least offer the possibility to divide domestic responsibilities more equitably. In short, intensification has the potential both to ease what are called space-time budgeting problems (where and when you do what) faced by women combining various roles and also to increase men's involvement at home.

Towards Intensification - And Towards Women-Friendly Cities

Proponents of intensification suggest that revising zoning by-laws and Official Plans is a first important step towards their overall goal. Many of these modifications also hold the promise of positive benefits for women. For example, zoning by-laws that privilege a narrow definition of the family limit the housing options available to non-traditional and non-heterosexual households. Low-income women (rates of poverty are higher among women than men, especially if they are lone mothers) are faced with a minuscule supply of legal, affordable housing. By precluding the sharing of a house with unrelated individuals, aged women cannot rent out part of their house to defray their housing costs which would allow them to remain in their community; and lone mothers cannot share with other lone mothers in order to divide their domestic responsibilities. This is why the recent legalization of accessory apartments in Ontario (Bill 120) was so significant for women. It is also why women's advocacy groups such as Women Plan Toronto have been lobbying to amend zoning by-laws and Official Plans so that they allow accessory apartments, mixed income housing and child-care facilities at workplaces. "Wouldn't it be nice," they argue, "if planners as part of their training had to live with a child for a day."

Some Notes of Caution

Home-based work receives a great deal of applause in the intensification debate. In some ways home-based work sounds like an great solution to many of the negative aspects of commuting (including environmental spill-over effects) and seems an ideal way to ease the strains of women's combined roles. For some it is. The popular image of homework is a well-paid, professional in their home-office connected to the outside world though a telephone, modem and fax machine. However, most women are not well-paid professionals even when they do commute to work. In fact, homeworking for some women might mean doing piece work for a garment company (which is on the increase again and notoriously poorly paid).

Intensification should produce neighbourhoods that are more supportive of lone mothers, who are less likely to have access to car, and more likely to be renters and in poverty than others. For a variety of reasons, lone mothers are disproportionately located downtown. However, over the last twenty years city neighbourhoods have undergone gentrification (rather than intensification), with the flipside being displacement and the loss of affordable housing. Increasingly, low-income lone mothers are being pushed out to suburban communities which do have high and medium density neighbourhoods (think about apartment buildings in North York and Scarborough), but do not provide a range of accessible services and facilities or even easy access to transit. So intensification has to involve more than density, it should also include accessible services. We need to be aiming for multi-use intensification rather than merely residential intensification. If intensification is not to have similar adverse impacts to those of gentrification, we need to keep asking ourselves "intensification for whom?"

Intensification must involve more than density, it should also include accessible services.

Does Sustainable Transportation mean Cities without Cars?

Richard Gilbert

If our transportation needs are to be met without compromising the ability of future generations to meet their own needs we may have to ban private automobiles from our urban areas. A recent study (*Cities without Cars*) funded by three federal government departments, managed by the Canadian Urban Institute, and involving planners and others in the Vancouver and Toronto regions examined how the two urban regions might function without cars in the early part of the 21st century. It was the first part of a two-part study and focused on land-use and transportation arrangements. (The second part of the study will address economic and social aspects of the *Cities without Cars* scenario, the specifics of possible implementation, and the use of the scenario as a tool for stimulating discussion about transportation and related matters.)

Sustainable development has become a catch-phrase of the 1990s. It was first used in the early 1980s, popularized by the 1987 report of the World Commission on Environment and Development (the Bruntland Commission), and was the main objective of the 1992 United Nations Conference on Environment and Development (UNCED) in Rio de Janeiro. UNCED adopted "Agenda 21," which states that the activities of the various sectors of society should develop in a sustainable way.

Sustainable development was defined by the Bruntland Commission as development that meets the needs of the present without compromising the ability of future generations to meet their own needs. Sustainable transportation (referred to as sustainable mobility by the European Commission) is proving to be the most elusive of the components of sustainable development. Emissions into the atmosphere from just about every other kind of human activity are being curbed; emissions from transportation are growing. Improvements in fuel efficiency and pollution control are being more than offset by growth in the ownership and use of motor vehicles.

Local pollution, congestion, and extravagant use of land are the main immediate focuses of concern about motor vehicle use, but for the medium and long term the main concern is emission of carbon dioxide and the ability of CO_2 to trap the sun's heat and produce global warming. The 300 or so experts that comprise the Intergovernmental Panel on Climate Change have concluded that CO_2 emissions from human activity will have to be reduced by 60 per cent or more in order to prevent potentially disastrous increases in the

global temperature. Just about all motorized transportation depends on the burning of fossil fuels, a major source of CO_2 emissions, and CO_2 emissions from transportation continue to grow at the rate of several per cent a year.

Such is the difficulty in achieving action to reduce motor vehicle use at local, regional, and national levels, necessary action may have to be international in nature, along the lines of the 1987 Montreal Protocol on Substances that Deplete the Ozone Layer and its subsequent annexes. The *Cities without Cars* study assumed that such international action would be taken with respect to motor vehicle use, specifically to require that use of private automobiles in urban regions around the world be phased out during the first few decades of the 21st century. The study did not question the validity of

Richard Gilbert is an urban issues consultant and past President of the Canadian Urban Institute. He is an urban transportation specialist for the Organization for Economic Cooperation and Development based in Paris, France, chairing their Expert Group on Sustainable Transportation.

Table 1. Land Use and Transportation Data for the Toronto and Vancouver Regions (1990)			
	Greater Toronto Area (GTA)	Greater Vancouver Regional District (GVRD)	GTA/ GVRD
Population	4,112,165	1,499,265	2.7
Employment	2,342,733	750,000	3.1
Employed persons/resident	0.57	0.50	
Land use characteristics			
Size of urbanized area (km^2)	1,536	1,200	1.3
Residential density (people/km^2)	2,677	1,249	2.1
Employment density (jobs/km^2)	1,525	625	2.4
Percentage of single-family homes	43	53	
Transportation system characteristics			
Car ownership (veh./1000 people)	463	444	1.0
Transit service (ann. veh-km/person)	62	58	1.1
Transit system average speed (km/h)	22	23	1.0
Road system average speed (km/h)	45	40	1.1
Annual transportation activity			
Automobile trips per person	536	632	0.8
Transit trips per person	131	97	1.4
Total motorized trips per person	667	729	0.9
Automobile trips per automobile	1,159	1,423	0.8
Average km travelled by each automobile	18,444	13,854	1.3
Automobile veh-km (millions)	35,116	9,222	3.8
Transit veh-km (millions)	245	71	3.5
Freight truck veh-km (millions)	6,637	1,743	3.8
Freight veh-km as % of all veh-km	15.8	15.8	
Automobile veh-km/person	8,540	6,151	1.4
Average automobile trip length (km)	15.9	9.7	1.6
Energy use for transportation (Mj/person)	47,891	36,103	1.3

Source: IBI Group, *Initiatives to limit transportation energy consumption and emissions in Canadian cities.* Prepared for Natural Resources Canada, September 1993.

the scenario. It assumed merely that urban regions without automobiles was a possible scenario worthy of investigation.

Teams of land-use and transportation planners and other urban specialists in Toronto and Vancouver worked over several months in late 1993 and early 1994 to develop principles, guidelines, and strategies for the reconfiguration of their regions so that comfort, convenience, and efficiency could be sustained in the absence of personal automobiles. Basic data on the two regions appear in the table on page 59.

After some initial skepticism, the teams concluded the following:

• To the extent we are serious about our vision of a sustainable future, the Cities without Cars scenario is more likely to achieve our objectives than the alternatives.

• The *Cities without Cars* scenario is desirable, possible, and even necessary.

• A car-free city would not necessarily have to be more dense than a city with cars, although intensification of development is generally desirable.

• A car-free city would likely spawn a diverse public-transit marketplace with many economic opportunities.

• The *Cities without Cars* scenario, compared with its alternatives, would provide better conditions for most of the objective measures of quality of life.

From the perspective of the Intensification Report the most interesting and challenging conclusion is the third one, which suggests - perhaps paradoxically - that intensification may be less necessary without automobiles than with them. The key to the puzzle is the insight, obvious when achieved, that public transport would be more viable at low densities of development if there were no competition from the automobile.

With present levels of automobile use, residential densities in excess of 6,000 per square kilometre over a wide area are required to sustain heavy-rail transit without insupportable subsidies; densities greater than 3,000/km² are required to sustain surface transit. Few parts of urban areas in North America exceed even 3,000/km². If most journeys were made by transit rather than by automobile, there would be at least three times as many transit trips per square kilometre, other things being equal. It follows that, to sustain transit, densities of no more than a third of presently needed levels would be required.

From a policy perspective there is thus an alternative to intensification. It is to restrict automobile use. But how might automobile use be restricted in the very low-density areas where the automobile is most needed? This conundrum is one of many to be addressed in Phase 2 of the *Cities without Cars* study.

The teams' conclusion that intensification is desirable even though it may not be necessary should also be stressed. The teams argued that even though it may not be required to support comprehensive transit services (although it would likely help), intensification is desirable to reduce the length of walking and bicycling trips, to increase accessibility generally, and to enhance the texture of communities, among many other reasons. ... however, a mixing of uses and functions may be more essential than density increases alone, although not necessarily to the point of developing self-contained communities within the urban region.

The most important conclusion of Phase 1 of the *Cities without Cars* study was that sustainable transportation may well require the banning of private automobiles in urban areas.

Note:
The funding of the study *Cities without Cars: An exploration of how two of Canada's large urban areas might cope with the disappearance of the private automobile in the early part of the 21st century: Report on Phase 1 (1994)*, was provided by the Ministry of Natural Resources, Environment Canada and Transportation Canada. This does not necessarily constitute support for the conclusions of the study.

Telecommunications Technologies: The Implications

Cities in the Information Age

Pamela Blais

Pamela Blais is President of Metropole Consulting Ltd. She is also a former Associate with Berridge Lewinberg Greengerg Dark Gabor, Ltd.

There are many visions of the city in the information age. Will we all be working from home, or cocooned in our electronic cottages in the mountains or by lakeside? Will the only communities be virtual communities? Does the information age spell the end of cities, allowing people and businesses to locate wherever they choose? Or does it represent a new basis for their revitalisation and a central role in the economy?

One thing is sure: the information revolution is the single most important force shaping cities today. Yet there is very little understanding or original research to shed light on how this is happening, and what results might be expected. Most of the investigation linking telecommunications to urban development has concerned the shift of work from the office to the home, tying this to the technology, and the changing organization of work.

The reality is much more far reaching, complex and subtle. If we want to understand the impacts of telecommunications and information on cities, we need to understand its underlying dynamics, and to do so more holistically. We also need to understand the full range of potential impacts on the city, which extend well beyond work-at-home. This article sketches such an approach, and suggests some areas of major impact on cities.

The Dynamics of Information Technology

Though chaotic, the information revolution does have an underlying logic, which is primarily an economic one. Information technology gives firms a decisive advantage in a competitive environment that demands high value-added goods and services, constant innovation, flexibility, and turn-on-a-dime responsiveness. Computer-assisted design and testing, instant inventory tracking, reduced need for retooling and downtime in manufacturing, detailed customer databases, global electronic capital transfer, infinite organizational options, are just a few examples of how information technology achieves the competitive edge.

The changing nature of competition has brought about major adjustments in the economy. There are three levels of change. At the level of the economy as a whole, there has been a loss of traditional manufacturing jobs and growth of the service sector. At the level of the firm or organization, there have been dramatic changes such as the multi-locational corporation, downsizing, the replacement of in-house capabilities with outside contractors, the rise of the small firm and the "network enterprise". Related to this is occupational change, and the explosion of the managerial class. In the Toronto Census Metropolitan Area (CMA), for example, managers, administrators and professionals grew from 25 per cent of total employment to 35 per cent between 1976 and 1990. Finally, at the level of the individual worker, we see the increasing precedence of part-time work, contract work, self-employment and informal sector employment. Related to these trends are home-based businesses, telecommuting, and neighbourhood telecentres. Computerization of the office has led to space-less accommodation of workers - the virtual corporation, the virtual office, or the automobile office. Corporations are also attacking office space requirements through innovative approaches such as "hotelling".

The city might be thought of as comprised of different types of puzzle pieces - neighbourhoods, shopping centres, downtowns, edge cities, or business parks - fitting together to form an urban whole. In assessing the potential impacts of the information revolution, however, it is more appropriate to begin not with these puzzle pieces as the basic unit of analysis, but with the economic dynamic that underlies it and, looking at each place in terms of its economic function and the role of information in the competitive dynamics of the sectors which are represented. For example, if we approach the downtown in terms of its economic role, then we can understand its likely future better. Toronto's financial core has recently suffered from reduced rents and high vacancy rates. Is this cyclical, related to the recession or structural, related to the information revolution?

At the level of the economy as a whole, financial services are a growth industry due to increased demand by an increasingly middle-aged (i.e. investor) population, deregulation and the broadening range, and quality of services that can be offered thanks to information technology itself. Financial services create jobs; and jobs (workers) are the source of demand for space. It is estimated that over 80 per cent of office employment is in the finance, insurance, real estate, and service industries (Wheaton, 1993).

While the financial services sector and employment seem poised to continue to grow, it is not at all clear whether this will translate into increased demand for office space in general, or demand for downtown office space particularly. The location of demand will depend in part on the type of employment. Financial services have created a large number of upper level and well paying jobs, as well as a large number of low paying, routine

administrative jobs, with relatively few middle-level opportunities. The former are likely to require core locations next to the action, word-of-mouth information, and specialized business services supported by a certain level of on-site clerical employees. But, as we have already seen, middle-level or routine information processing jobs have been exported out of the high-cost core to low-cost "back office" locations in the suburbs, exurbs, or to other countries.

Employment increases may be offset by more efficient use of office space. Ernst and Young recently demonstrated the viability of this approach by reducing their space requirements on Seventh Avenue in New York City from 250 to 100 square feet per employee, through a combination of innovative space management techniques and information technology.

Putting all these factors together, the financial core function will continue in the downtown, but the growth of the sector itself and employment will not translate directly into demand for central office space. The core will consist only of those high-level professionals who require the central location, and the minimum of staff required to support them. The office space they consume will be minimized through efficient space management techniques. If it is to remain viable, the idea of the downtown will have to be rethought, and the place itself diversified, to become a cultural, shopping, living and working centre rather than a "financial core".

The Dimensions of Cyber-City

The impacts of the information revolution are not, of course, limited to the downtown. There are a variety of potential implications, at all scales.

The City-System

Certain kinds of cities will grow and certain kinds of cities will not. Urban fortunes will depend upon a place's position in the global information economy, the urban hierarchy, and the local attractions it can offer to attract information-based businesses or residents.

... the idea of the downtown will have to be rethought, and the place itself diversified to become a cultural, shopping, living and working centre rather than a "financial core".

Patterns of urban growth and development

Does the information revolution herald a renewed era of urban sprawl, or does it provide new impetus for concentration? Will there be any reason at all to continue to segregate cities into districts, according to their use?

The internal organization of the city

Each urban puzzle piece must be analyzed according to its own logic.

• The information revolution opens up new possibilities for viable reurbanisation, the re-use of derelict land and unused industrial buildings. These buildings are ideally suited for living and working in the same unit, and are already (often illegally) used for such purposes, suggesting a strong demand. With work-at-home, the redesignation of industrial land for residential purposes may result in more on-site jobs than would be possible from maintaining an industrial designation.

• Older downtowns and financial centres are likely to be impacted, as well (though likely in a different way) as new suburban centres - nascent and planned. The viability of the GTA's "nodal" growth concept, based on a multitude of concentrated office employment nodes, may be overestimated.

• In retail areas, the current bane of planners - the big box stores and power centres - are likely to be impacted as interactive home shopping becomes more of a reality.

• And of course, the neighbourhood is poised for dramatic change, as more and more people work at home and require business services and other amenities closer to their homes. Existing neighbourhoods will have to adapt to these changes or decline.

• Finally, the design of new communities will change to cater to these new realities of integrating work, live and play spaces in new types of urban environments.

Urban management

Infotech can be used to better manage the administration and maintenance of cities, and municipal services. This includes a need to re-examine the methods and mechanisms of urban planning and land use control. Regulations which separate home from work, or different types of employment areas from each other become less relevant and even counter-productive. A plethora of potential applications includes electronic road pricing (a pilot project is underway in Cambridge, England) and computerized traffic management.

Urban economic development

Not only does infotech level the playing field, giving Corner Brook, Newfoundland a more even chance to compete against Toronto, but there is a whole range of potential new tools. Croydon, England, has adopted a local economic development strategy which aims to make it a "European Telecommunications City". The strategy has several priority projects, including a Local Area Network (LAN) called "Croydon On-Line", which links businesses with each other and with government, institutions, and on-line information services to improve competitiveness.

In Canada, with one of the most advanced telecommunications infrastructures in the world, it's time to mine our creativity, tap this valuable resource, and start planning cities for the current and future information age.

> Not only does infotech level the playing field, giving Corner Brook, Newfoundland a more even chance to compete against Toronto, but there is a whole range of potential new tools.

The Challenge for Public Transit in the Telecommunications Age

Francis Frisken

These are difficult times for transportation planners and public transit operators. On the one hand they are urged by environmentalists and neotraditional planners to revise their thinking about the way cities and urban regions will develop, and to plan for denser, more compact urban settlements geared to walking, cycling and public transit. On the other hand, data on travel trends, buttressed by the arguments of those who foresee no reversal in the outward spread of urban settlements, dictate a continuing need to accommodate automobiles while treating other transportation modes as being of lesser and declining importance. Among those promoting the latter view are persons convinced that new telecommunications technologies will enable the majority of urban residents to work, shop and access all forms of entertainment out of their homes, thereby reducing the need to travel and allowing people greater latitude in choosing where to live.

The impacts of new technologies on both work and travel patterns are still matters for speculation, much of which fails to take account of the importance most human beings assign to interpersonal interactions in ordering their daily lives. It also tends to focus on those types of jobs performed by persons who are not only highly-skilled in the use of telecommunications technologies but are also able to adapt on their own to rapid advances in the field. It is these persons who are best able to take advantage of the freedom to reside where they choose, with little thought to daily travel needs. The individuals who can do so most easily, in fact, are persons living in households with only one member gainfully employed, or in which all employed members can work at home. For the many urban residents who still depend on traditional types of work - in manufacturing, for example (where jobs have been declining as a

proportion of total employment, but not in absolute numbers), or in personal or community services - technological change may mean having to learn new skills, but it is unlikely to reduce the need to travel. The growing number of persons who hold more than one job, or who participate in adult education programs, may in fact have to make more rather than fewer daily trips in order to adapt to economic and technological change.

Even though telecommunications technologies are unlikely to reduce and may even increase the need for urban travel, they may contribute indirectly to reducing transportation choices for urban residents. A feature of the new technologies is that they allow public agencies and private firms to locate all or most of their activities away from the urban core and high density, transit-accessible nodes, in the interest of minimizing rents and taxes, while keeping them in constant communication with head offices and ancillary services. Consequently, proliferation of these technologies is likely to accelerate tendencies that have characterized urban regions for an extended period of time: a leveling off or even decline in the rate of population growth in core cities, together with rapid population growth in low density suburbs. These trends are making many urban destinations - for employment and other purposes- non-central, isolated even from their immediate surroundings, and often difficult to access by public transit. Not surprisingly, then, use of public transit for all purposes is much lower in the suburbs than in core cities. As dispersal has increased, use of public transit has also been declining, relative to automobile use, in both core cities and their suburbs.

Public policy has played a role in promoting both the land use patterns that influence current urban travel and the

Fances Frisken is a Professor in the Urban Studies Program in the Social Sciences Department at York University.

degree of modal choice that still exists in Canada's metropolitan areas. Public policies have been working at cross purposes, in other words. Permissive provincial laws and regulations have allowed suburban governments to give preference to single family homes on sizable lots, accessible only by convoluted street patterns and segregated from other types of land use, without giving thought to their likely consequences for urban transportation. On the other hand, both provincial and municipal subsidies have made it possible for transit operators to run buses into or close to such areas, despite the relatively low level of transit use they generate. Nonetheless, the bulk of transit subsidies has gone either into construction and operation of high speed rapid transit facilities designed to enhance accessibility to, and thereby promote office/commercial development in, central areas and high density suburban nodes, or into providing bus services to carry suburban commuters downtown or to rapid transit terminals.

Canadian governments have begun to acknowledge contradictions inherent in past transportation policies in widely-different ways. So far the most transit supportive response has come from the government of Ontario, which has not only sponsored the production and distribution of Transit-Supportive Land Use Planning Guidelines (Ontario Ministry of Transportation and Ministry of Municipal Affairs, 1992) but is also preparing to make changes in its Planning Act to encourage (though not compel) municipal governments to accept more compact, higher density forms of development containing a mixture of land uses and housing types. At the other extreme is the Quebec government's decision to end virtually all operating subsidies to local transit (while retaining full right to decide when, where and whether new rapid transit will be built). It has thereby made individual municipal governments responsible for deciding not only whether their own residents can choose among alternative modes of travel but also whether destinations in their communities will be accessible to transit users in other parts of the region.

While the Ontario approach commends itself to those calling for more environmentally-sensitive urban development practices, that of the Quec government is more consistent with current political realities. Having worked hard to persuade voters of the urgent need for spending cuts and debt reduction, governments now find it difficult to justify policies that fail to reduce the problem (e.g., road congestion) they purport to address. Unless politicians and their publics perceive public transit as playing an essential role in local transportation, they will not support it. For transit to play such a role, it must begin to address a serious and growing deficiency in urban transportation systems - their inability to move urban residents from one suburban district to another without forcing them to make convoluted, time-consuming journeys.

Changing the way we plan and design residential communities is a first step toward making cities and urban regions more hospitable to transit. It is unrealistic, however, to expect new planning approaches to produce noticeable changes in urban travel habits in the immediate future. It has taken more than half a century to produce the metropolitan areas that exist today; it is likely to take just as long to alter them significantly, even where there is a will to do so. So far it has been easier to incorporate neotraditional concepts into plans for entirely new residential districts in outer suburbs than to gain their acceptance for already-built-up areas, where higher densities are probably needed just to maintain transit use at existing levels.

Residential districts planned on neotraditional lines will be easier to serve with transit, but they will also put transit in competition with walking and cycling for many local trips. Thus their principal outcome, from a public transit perspective, will be to make it easier for transit operators to link new suburban districts to rapid transit stations. Indirectly, therefore, they will help increase transit connections to a limited number of urban destinations - particularly urban downtowns and districts surrounding or within relatively short bus rides of transit terminals. They are unlikely to make it easier to provide fast and convenient service between residential districts and the growing number of suburban destinations providing employment, educational (including retraining), and recreational opportunities, as well as a broad range of social and community services.

Transportation planners and transit operators have largely ignored the challenge of enhancing rapid transit connections to and among suburban locations both because of their high construction and operating costs and because it is difficult to persuade policy-makers that such facilities are likely to bring immediate political or economic benefits. Failure to address this challenge, however, implies a steady decline in public transit use and the probable loss of transit service in all but the more heavily built up parts of urban regions. Such a loss will bring

social as well as environmental costs. Transit accessible locations are likely to specialize in those activities (like high-paying office jobs and costly forms of mass entertainment) that attract persons who can choose easily among alternative transportation modes, and who do so primarily on the basis of speed and convenience. Less accessible locations will attract a larger proportion of those who have few choices as to where and how they will live and where and how they will work. Faced with a decline in transportation options, such persons will have to decide between curtailing their travel, thereby limiting their opportunities still further, and buying and operating a car, thereby reducing the amount of money they have to spend for housing and other necessities. Both choices imply reduced capacity to participate in and contribute to the urban economy.

Telework and its Impact on Urban Form

Penny Gurstein

It is estimated that over two million Canadians - nearly one-quarter of the working population - do some or all of their paid labour at home. While this growing trend is having a major impact on Canadian society it has largely been ignored as a factor in the planning of communities. Residential planning based on the principle of separating home and work activities is clearly outdated, and needs to be rethought in light of contemporary social and economic conditions. To this end, the Canada Mortgage and Housing Corporation (CMHC) funded study "Planning for Telework and Home-Based Employment: A Canadian Survey on Integrating Work into Residential Environments," investigates the impact that telework and home-based employment has on the use of the home and neighbourhood, and the implications for the planning and design of homes and communities.

The study was designed as a mail-out survey that obtained detailed data on:

characteristics of the household; work profile of the home-based worker; community context of the household (i.e., services and ambiance of neighbourhood, usage patterns, modes of transportation, regulatory restrictions); spatial organization of the home; spatial organization of the work site (i.e., size, layout, amenities, special requirements); telecommunications usage for work; and, the role of the home and community to the home-based worker. The sample for the survey included teleworkers who work for public institutions, crown corporations or the private sector, independent contractors who work on contract to one company, self-employed consultants, and home-based business operators. The Canada-wide response rate was 31 per cent.

Of those surveyed close to half (48 per cent) described themselves as self-employed consultants or home-based business operators, and one-third (31 per cent) described themselves as public sector, crown corporation or private sector

Penny Gurstein is a Professor in the School of Community and Regional Planning and a Faculty Research Associate at the Centre for Human Settlements, University of British Columbia, specializing in urban design and the socio-cultural aspects of community planning.

This article was drawn from a report on the planning and design implications of telework and home-based employment, produced for the Canada Mortgage and Housing Corporation.

teleworker. While the catchment area of the sample did not include supplementers (i.e., an employee who brings work home on an occasional basis), 13 per cent of the respondents typified themselves as moonlighters, occasional homeworkers or "other." Finally, 8 per cent were independent contractors who work on contract to one company. These figures are comparable to the estimates developed in a 1992 study by Orser and Foster for the Home-Based Business Project Committee which investigated the nature and extent of home-based business activity in Canada which estimated that 48 per cent of home-based workers are self-employed, and the rest are either supplementers or substituters such as teleworkers.

An at-home worker is more likely to have a professional or business occupation if he or she lives in British Columbia, Ontario or Quebec. If they live in the Prairies or Atlantic Canada they are more likely to have occupations that involve manufacturing or processing of crafts and retail sales. Home-based workers most likely have worked in their occupation for over 10 years, but at home in their occupation for under 5 years. On average they work over 40 hours per week.

Distinct patterns emerge between teleworkers and other home-based workers. Teleworkers are better educated and have a larger annual household income than other home-based workers. Teleworkers generally work part-time at home, going to corporate offices for meetings, and to confer with superiors and colleagues. Self-employed consultants and home-based business operators travel a considerable amount for their work, visiting clients and associates. Independent contractors almost exclusively work at home, travelling only to deliver completed work and obtain new projects. Almost all of the home-based workers have a computer to conduct their home-based work activities, and regularly use a fax machine. A sizeable number (mostly teleworkers) also regularly use electronic mail and computer networks.

The majority of home-based workers, similar to other Canadians, live in single family detached homes in suburban communities or urban areas built in the last 40 years. The home is used primarily by at-home workers for administration and providing services. Almost all of the workers have a designated workspace at home, but two-thirds have to share this space with other activities. Female home-based workers with children in particular select their workspace so that they can monitor family activities. Some of the major problems with working at home include lack of storage for materials and products, and intrusions from family, neighbours and friends. Generally, to be successful working at home workers have to have an organized workspace with clear boundaries between work and household spaces.

Many at-home workers have done modifications to their home to make it suitable for work. These include renovations, rewiring and cosmetic treatment such as painting. Those with disabilities have found it necessary to retrofit their homes to make them suitable. Home-based workers have a definite idea of their ideal type of workspace. It includes a separate room for the workspace, natural lighting and ventilation, visual and acoustical privacy, and adequate storage and electrical amperage and outlets. Opinions vary about the ideal home for home-based work, and where it would be located. Nevertheless, many home-based workers recognize that having their work located in their home affords them the ability to choose a home and its location based on a set of priorities that allow for the integration of both home and work.

Home-based workers have not appreciably changed their use of their neighbourhood since working at home, nor do they interact with their neighbours more in significant numbers. They do generally feel, though, that working at home enhances the security of their home and neighbourhood. As well, for some home-based workers their community has become a great source of friendship and support. Working at home does not change the preferred mode of transportation but it does significantly decrease the distance spent travelling for all activities. Particularly for teleworkers, their automobile use has significantly decreased.

Home-based workers generally feel that the municipal regulations governing their occupations are too restrictive. These regulations do not reflect the nature of most of their work which is of a non-toxic, non-hazardous nature and rarely has a major negative impact on the functioning of their neighbourhoods. It appears that many home-based workers feel that they are treated unfairly by their municipalities and want a revamping of zoning and regulations to more accurately reflect the nature of their work.

Over one-quarter of the home-based workers would be interested in working from a neighbourhood telework centre or satellite office. They see the advantages of being close to home without the distractions they find working at home, and would appreciate the services and camaraderie that such centres would provide.

In the sample for this study, home-based work is perceived very positively by those who work at home. It provides flexibility and control over work, allowing more of a integration between home and work life. Female home-based workers with families particularly appreciate the opportunity that home-based work affords to maintain their family responsibilities. Male home-based workers particularly appreciate the control over their work and daily schedule. Teleworkers were very satisfied with their opportunity to work at home and believed that their productivity has increased. They also seem to be satisfied that working at home will not have undue consequences for their career opportunities and interactions with managers and co-workers.

The disadvantages are maintaining a healthy balance between home and work life, and the lack of social interactions. Female home-based workers find balancing family and work responsibilities particularly problematic. In general however, the advantages considerably outweigh the disadvantages for most home-based workers.

Telework and home-based employment is unlikely to generate a return to wide-spread locally-based community life as envisioned by some theorists. The phenomenon, nevertheless, may enhance the desirability of the neighbourhood as a locale for work-related services and as a respite from the intensity of home/work spaces. Neighbourhood telework centers allow opportunities for working in close proximity to the home using shared office space and services. Other services such as cafes, bookstores, and copy shops may be generated by the use of these centers. In addition, the importance of the neighbourhood as a sensory relief from the sterility of staring into a computer screen all day cannot be overlooked. The siting and landscaping of neighbourhoods to provide opportunities for a pleasurable walking or biking experience take on added significance for home-based workers.

Given the non-toxic and non-intrusive nature of most home-based work activities and its increasing importance as a work option, there is considerable justification to revamp existing by-laws regarding home occupations to make them less restrictive in residential zones. This, in turn, could encourage more innovative solutions to incorporating working at home or close to home such as co-housing projects with community workspaces, backyard studios/offices, and community work centres with support services and technologies for the beginning entrepreneur. As well, increasingly homes will be wired with the same capabilities as office settings, effectively blurring the distinction between home and work.

Clearly new work options and the telecommunications technologies to support these options will allow more choices in ways of living and working, resulting in changes in social and spatial relationships. These technologies will allow geographical dispersal, but they will also allow the promotion of local specialized communities based on common interests. People will have the possibility of doing most of their production and consumption activities in their home, but there will still be the need for face-to-face contacts. As with other technologies, these technologies open up a myriad of possibilities for weakening and reshaping communities and the urban form of cities.

Home-based workers generally feel that the municipal regulations governing their occupations are too restrictive.

Innovative Development Practices: The New Urbanism

Village of Morrison: Community Building Practices

Marvin Green

Marvin Green is the President of the River Oaks Group, consultants in urban development and design.

Postwar suburban planning and development have generated an environment that is now all too familiar to most of us. Our suburbs, and many parts of our cities, have become automobile-dependent places that are expensive to build and maintain, socially isolating, and environmentally questionable.

Efforts to reinforce the urban characteristics of our cities are under way with varying degrees of success. In the last few years however, many people have also turned their attention to the building of new suburban places with greater care, and with reformed ideas on the environment, transportation, household composition, economics, and aesthetics. Many development proposals are now under way that challenge conventional patterns in fundamental ways. The proponents of such proposals are obliged to demonstrate to local planners, engineers, and councillors a host of reasons why changes to current practice are needed and timely. Deeply entrenched thought patterns and methods are not easily altered, yet there is great movement in some places.

Perhaps the first such plan to receive full approval in Ontario is the Village of Morrison in Oakville. The developer, the River Oaks Group, has engaged a team of consultants including Berridge Lewinberg Greenberg Ltd., Hough, Stansbury, Woodland Ltd., Cosburn, Patterson Wardman Ltd., and Entra Ltd. A vibrant and highly interactive process was developed to analyze the problems of conventional suburban development and seek creative ways to build communities that can respond to these problems. The plan that has emerged is one that is beneficial to the natural environment, pedestrian and cyclist friendly, supportive of public transit, and economical in both the short and long term; it challenges conventional development standards.

On January 11, 1993, Oakville Town council approved the zoning bylaw and draft plan of subdivision for the Village of Morrison. The 6.3-hectare, wedge shaped site is bordered by Morrison Creek to the east, the new 6th Line Road to the west, and the Trans-Canada Pipeline corridor to the south. Up to 192 residential units will be built on the site at a density of 60 units per net hectare. This represents significant land savings that will reduce the cost of the housing and the outward pressure on farmland at the fringe of the urban area.

The developer and associated builders have engaged four architects to design single-detached, semi-detached, row houses and small multiplex apartment buildings. Narrow frontage lots in the Village of Morrison plan vary in width from 5.5 metres for row houses to 9 metres for single detached houses; they are roughly 30 metres in depth. Public laneways are provided for access to private parking at the rear of all lots. In October 1992, the Oakville Council voted to accept these laneways as public infrastructure to be owned and maintained by the municipality. The provision of parking at the rear frees he front of the house from the typical garage presentation. Rather than being dominated by garage doors and characterized by a lack of windows and confusing, often hidden entranceways, the Village of Morrison houses will be fronted by porches, have ample space for fenestration, and be comprehensible as street oriented components in the building and organization of the community.

The Village of Morrison will closely integrate a mix of housing types, architectural "styles," and forms of tenure. This is in contrast to typical suburban development in which streets are organized by lot width, where, for example, large areas are composed exclusively of 18- or 20-metre lots and large houses. Streets in Toronto's Rosedale neighbourhood exhibit a fine example of well integrated building types, yet are considered desirable places to live.

The units vary in floor area from less than 170 to nearly 300 square metres. Economically priced condominium units in the small multiplex buildings will be accessible to lower-income households normally excluded from the real estate market. Generic and highly streamlined documents have been prepared to greatly reduce the legal costs normally associated with creating condominium units and corporations This alone will bring down the price of the units. Houses with three parking spaces will allow for the creation of accessory units. Rental stock will be created and rental income will make the purchase of a home possible for more people.

Many Canadian households contain income-producing activities. Accordingly, provisions have been made to allow Village of Morrison residents to create home offices and small studios. The zoning bylaw and site design have made possible the construction of accessory units at the rear of the properties, usually on a second floor over the parking area. The wide variety of housing types, tenure forms, and possible accessory units provide much choice to purchasers and renters. The diversity of

Site plan for the Village of Morrison

options and the range of people expected to live in 6th Line should make it a vibrant place to live.

Conventional storm water management techniques are designed to remove rain water from public and private property as soon as possible. By measure of highly engineered systems, including extensive paving, grading, catch basins, sewer pipes, and containment structures, water is removed so quickly that a generation of children have been raised without much experience of puddles or mud. But these engineered systems have degraded the quality of water courses and lowered ground water tables. The first effect is caused by fast moving water-borne pollution being deposited in the water course. (The water has been warmed and polluted by contact with roads and roofs.) This alters and destroys aquatic and plant life as well as causing significant shoreline alteration. The second effect is caused by the redirection of water rather than allowing it to sink into the ground and to recharge the water table below. Storm water in the easterly half of the site is to be conveyed overland towards Morisson Creek rather than in sewers. A wetland area is be created en route to the creek as a natural means to improve water quality before final release into the water course. Storm water quantity controls are to be constructed at various points on the site. These will include at-source means such as cisterns (for re-use of rain water), underground infiltration galleries, and landscaping and planting to encourage both recharge and plant uptake of moisture. A linear park will be used to direct storm water to Moroccan Creek. By means such as these, the use of expensive and environmentally intrusive storm sewer pipe will be greatly reduced.

The Village of Morrison is designed to be pedestrian and cyclist friendly. Houses are placed close to the street edge to define a public realm that is recognizable and protected from harsh climatic conditions. Front door to opposing front door distances will be in the order of 22 metres, in contrast to the approximately 40 metres found in most new suburban streets. Streets and laneways will be connected to each other and the existing community in a grid pattern to create easily navigable routes. A grid allows destinations to be reached in many different ways. Walking and cycling are more pleasurable and interesting when there is

the possibility of taking different routes on different days and experiencing a neighbourhood in many ways. Housing built at densities of 35 to 40 or so units per hectare on connected streets, such as those in 6th Line, can yield sufficient ridership to support public transit. Residential densities associated with conventional suburbs cannot do so.

Road rights-of-way are to be 16 metres in width, rather than the conventional 20 metres while pavement widths will be the usual eight metres. Sanitary sewers and some of the other utilities will be located in the seven metre laneway. The project engineers have done extensive research into the cost of producing and maintaining public infrastructure. They have shown that at the Village of Morrison densities, revenues from residential taxes more than offset costs associated with the public ownership and maintenance of laneways. These findings seem common sense, but constitute original and important research towards the acceptance of reformed community building practices.

The Village of Morrison plan includes a corner store on the central green. A corner store can help to alleviate the "litre of gas per litre of milk syndrome." In the Village of Morrison people will be able to walk to the store for routine purchases rather than being obligated to drive. Typical suburban strip plazas are dreary places, especially when stores are vacant. Corner store zoning allows the main floor of a house structure to be converted from residential to commercial use or the inverse with out major disruption. If no market exists for store use, the commercial portion will not stand idle or decay, but rather be re-integrated into the house as residential space.

In conventional suburbs with segregated housing types and monolithic demographic profiles, one discovers that most households generate the same number of students, of similar ages at the same time. Quite typically, new neighbourhood schools are filled to capacity only two years after opening in new subdivisions. After fifteen years the school population has peaked and then dwindles to the point where some school boards are then found scrambling to justify their existence. In the Village of Morrison project it is expected that a broad range of people will be resident. Seniors, singles, couples, traditional and non-traditional families will all reside in close proximity. As in mature neighbourhoods, it is expected that student generation will be relatively constant over time. This will allow for the planning and utilization of school facilities on a much more dependable basis. This should be both socially and economically beneficial to the community.

The Village of Morrison project has attempted to address a wide variety of issues relevant to suburban densification. It will be closely studied by governments, professionals, rate-payer groups, academics and others. Site servicing will begin in the spring of 1993 and the project should be complete by the end of 1993 or early 1994.

Editor's note: The Village of Morrison project is well underway, with over 100 houses built as of the summer of 1996.

Is the Neotraditional "Revolution" Likely to Occur?

Frank Clayton

The legacy that the current neo-traditional planning movement (or New Urbanism in the latest lexicon) will leave for future generations of Canadians will take at least one of three forms: an addition to the menu of housing choices now being offered to the buying and renting public (e.g., conventional subdivisions and planned communities); a revolutionary change in the way people live, work and shop reminiscent of pre-car towns and villages; or enhancements which improve the aesthetics and livability of choices currently available in the new housing market.

Supporters of the neo-traditional model see it as the panacea to many of society's current malaises - pollution, traffic congestion, lack of neighbourliness, and inefficient and costly land use patterns. In their view, only if we make fundamental changes to the way urban areas are planned and developed do we have the chance to offer future generations a better way of life.

I do not foresee the planning revolution touted by the neo-traditional supporters: the underlying premise of integrated land uses where people live, work and shop in the same community is not workable. What I do see is a new type of housing and living environment which is not being offered in the marketplace (with minor exceptions) which will appeal to a segment of (but by no means most) new home buyers. I also anticipate that the developers of conventional subdivisions will increasingly seek to adopt many of the design and site planning features of the neo-traditional model, e.g., narrower streets and smaller front yards, in response to competitive market pressures.

What worries me most about the neo-traditional proponents, especially those in positions of power in government is that, in their misguided enthusiasm, they endeavour to "force" all new development to follow the tenets of the neo-traditional approach. This could have serious undesirable consequences on housing costs and economic growth.

Will People Live In A Neo-Traditional Community?

Despite all the hype about neo-traditional planning over the past decade, there are actually few communities on the market in North America which incorporate neo-traditional principles. Seaside, the photogenic community on the Florida Panhandle, has more in common with fanciful tourist attractions like Disney

Frank Clayton is President of Clayton Research Associates Ltd., an economic consulting firm with offices in Toronto, Vancouver, Edmonton and Halifax, specializing in real estate market analysis and urban growth management.

World than a permanent place to live, work and shop. Its a vacation paradise for the wealthy. Similarly, a visit to Kentlands (in Maryland just outside Washington), the first on-the-ground neo-traditional community in a "northern location", suggested it is attracting upper income buyers not the mix of buyers that planners hyped for.

A recent survey of four neo-traditional communities in the United States (Harbortown in Memphis and Leguna West in Sacramento as well as Seaside and Kentlands) conducted by Market Perspectives, a California-based market research firm, provides some interesting insight into the buyers of neo-traditional homes (the data highlighted in the accompanying chart exclude Seaside where only five per cent of the owners live year-round).

It is evident that the buyers in the neo-traditional communities surveyed are only a select component of the home-buying public. They have relatively high incomes and few children. Most are repeat buyers. Few use the home as their primary workplace. Slightly less than 30 per cent of buyers have the much-publicized flat above a garage at the rear of the main house (and only a few of these buyers have put the flat on the rental market).

What do these buyers like about the neo-traditional community? A stronger sense of "neighbourliness" than in other subdivisions (68 per cent), preference for a front porch (69 per cent), minimum setbacks from the street (69 per cent), and narrower streets (61 per cent) are among the more important features.

For neo-traditional communities to become the norm in new community development, the buyer (and renter) profile will have to be broadened enormously. Is this likely? At the present time, buyers are paying a premium to live in a neo-traditional setting. This is because development and building costs are higher than for a conventional subdivision. The costs of a neo-traditional home must become competitive with more conventional developments if there is to be a more diverse buyer base.

In my opinion we will see a number of neo-traditional housing developments built across Canada which will appeal to a broader spectrum of buyers than the buyers to date. However, it is much more likely that developers and builders will be incorporating the more saleable features of the neo-traditional concept into their otherwise conventional developments. The widespread introduction of neo-traditional communities is not in the cards even if they do not incorporate the integration of housing with shopping and workplaces - which most will not.

Will People Shop On Main Street?

One of the underlying principles of neo-traditional planning is that most community-based services, including retailing, are within a short walk for residents with far less reliance on the automobile.

In its purist form, neo-traditional retail facilities are oriented to the street, typically with facades built right to the sidewalk. Parking areas are usually restricted to the back of a shopping area or in parking structures away from the main entrances which are intended for pedestrians. On-street parking is encouraged. Shop sizes are generally small and are configured in the street and block pattern. In many cases, planned retail uses are vertically integrated with affordable apartments above storefronts.

I have concluded that generally the pure neo-traditional retailing form is unworkable in suburban locations and not in the best interests of consumers, retailers or investors (see sidebar).

Full-line supermarkets (e.g., 35,000 square feet), for example, need the equivalent of more than 10,000 persons to do all their shopping there.

Inclement weather (e.g., Canadian winters), large purchases which are too difficult to walk with and time constraints are among the reasons why the automobile will continue to be, by far, the most popular mode of shopping transportation.

High volume retailers, as well as any large anchor tenant such as a department

... buyers in the neo-traditional communities surveyed ... have relatively high incomes and few children.

... buyers are paying a premium to live in a neo-traditional setting.

store, are difficult if not impossible to accommodate in a neo-traditional shopping area. Neo-traditional community residents are forced outside their community to do this type of shopping.

The ideal of a larger-scale new suburban main street to serve the day-to-day and ongoing needs of the local community has not materialized anywhere in North America. Examples of successful larger-scale retail facilities developed in a neo-traditional manner are in either high demand specialty retail areas or more closely resemble hybrids with conventional shopping centre components.

Mashpee Commons on Cape Cod is often cited as a successful neo-traditional shopping area, but it clearly benefits from being in a tourist area for specialty shopping. Furthermore, a conventional neighbourhood centre was developed adjacent to Mashpee Commons, to which the local food store relocated and expanded. Another neo-traditional example is Princeton Forrestal Village in New Jersey. The village shopping centre is only part of a 1,750 acre office/research park and is intended to serve local employees. The project has not been very successful due in part to poor visibility/image from the expressway (U.S. Route 1) and the lack of anchor tenants.

Some plans for neo-traditional retailing recognize the need for a conventional component. Carma Developers' McKenzie Towne community in Calgary will include a conventional strip plaza with access and visibility to a major arterial road to complement the adjacent main street commercial corridor. Moreover, two vital anchors are at the ends of main street, an LRT station and a large lake, which are intended to act as a catalyst to draw people and business to the main street.

Will Employers Locate In Neo-Traditional Communities?

Job opportunities within the neo-traditional setting are an even weaker link than retailing. It is not clear just what types of jobs will be attracted to the community and where they will be located.

Some proponents suggest that many of the jobs will be located in a mixed-use area, e.g., in offices above main street stores. Others look to the rapidly changing technology and the growth of home offices and businesses to create many jobs. Still others want to promote a sustainable community in which many of the services and products demanded by residents will be produced in a business park adjacent to the residential areas.

A recent study done for the Office of the Greater Toronto Area ("The Outlook For Population and Employment in the GTA", Hemson Consulting Ltd. and The Coopers & Lybrand Consulting Group, August, 1993) predicts that the bulk of new jobs in the future will be created in low-density buildings in suburban business parks. This underlying trend in the location of employment growth in the coming years is not reconcilable with the desire of the neo-traditionalists to have people walking, cycling (in good weather only I presume), and taking transit to their place of work.

Moreover, wage-earners change jobs more frequently than homeowners move. Thus, even if an earner were to locate in a given neo-traditional community because of a job there, the likelihood is that at some point this person will change jobs and have a workplace outside the community - often requiring use of a car.

Conclusion

Community planning, like virtually everything in this day and age, is in continual flux. Opportunities are created by responding to unsatisfied market needs. However, if changes attempt to aggressively alter human behaviours, they become much riskier.

The rise of the neo-traditional planning school of thought has made an important contribution, even if the future changes in land use planning and development practices occur at the margin and the complete revolution never occurs. Unquestionably, households and businesses should have the opportunity to locate in a neo-traditional setting. But this choice should be governed by the marketplace and not government edict.

Concerns about neotraditional planning retailing proposals: - not enough people live within a short walk to support larger-scale retailing - the automobile will always be an important part of most shpping trips - current retail trends ("big box" retailers) are contrary to neotraditional planning dictates.

Designer Suburbs

Hok-Lin Leung

Hok-Lin Leung is a Professor in the School of Urban and Regional Planning at Queen's University.

People seek environments that are congruent to their images of the ideal. But aspirations differ between the social and economic elite and the common people. Since ancient Greek and Roman times the elite has always desired the suburbs. In the second half of the 19th century, extreme urban congestion and uncontrolled industrial pollution, combined with improved transportation and rising incomes, made it desirable and possible for the urban elite to find refuge in the suburbs. These early suburbs were small, seldom accommodating more than 10,000 people, and were clustered neatly around the train stations that were spaced three to five miles apart, each surrounded by country greenery.

The common people did not and could not move. But suburban living became their environmental ideal. The end of World War II saw an economic boom: steady jobs, shorter working hours, and better wages. There was also a baby-boom. These, together with the mass production and use of the automobile, ushered in a period of unprecedented suburban expansion. The American dream of your own home in the suburbs was being realized by the newly affluent lower-middle and working classes.

In the last 30 years or so the image of good living for the elite has changed. At first there was a resentment to the invasion of the suburbs by the lower classes. Then there was a reevaluation of the suburban ideal. Suburb became "suburbia": a twilight zone - a sprawl of look-alike single-detached houses, aesthetically displeasing, environmentally irresponsible, and socially blase.

New environmental ideals for the elite have begun to emerge. One of them is the desire to move further out into exurbia where the lots are larger, nature more abundant, and the locale more prestigious. The rage, though, is "designer suburbs" which seek to recreate the "ambience" of the 19th century American small town. At the same time, the idea of inner-city living has re-entered the competition for the heart of the elite. "Higher density" living is making a comeback, whether it is the Seaside, Florida-type neo-traditional suburbs or the gentrified inner-city enclaves.

An interesting question arises. Will this "new urbanism" become the new environmental ideal of the masses?

Conventionally, we associate dwelling types with density, and density with crowding. For instance, typical net density (that is, the number of dwelling units for a given built-up area, excluding streets, public facilities and open spaces) is 20 per hectare for single-detached houses, 50 for rowhouses, 160 for three-storey walk-up apartments, and 300 for high-rise apartments. It also follows that higher densities mean more crowding, and greater loss of sunlight, space and privacy.

"New urbanism" represents a radical departure from the above conventional wisdom. As an ideology it sees the private plot with deep setbacks and large yards as a symbol of social disengagement and environmental irresponsibility. It affirms the urban street and communal open space as the glue that binds the good society. As a design approach it forsakes the conventions of "privacy through separation distances" and uses site layout, building orientation, fenestrations and materials to achieve visual and audio privacy.

Governments are placing great hopes on these "higher density" approaches as models of affordable housing for the growing number of citizens who can never hope to own a conventional suburban single detached home because of its rising prices and their dwindling incomes. Environmental interests see compact development as the basis of sustainable communities. But is this "new urbanism" affordable and sustainable?

The "higher" densities of the designer suburbs do not necessarily translate into lower housing costs. The dwelling types (more attached houses and smaller lots) and layouts (narrower streets and smaller setbacks) may suggest compactness. But we should not confuse built form with density. The built-up part is often surrounded by, or interspersed with, generous open spaces. This makes the actual land consumption much higher than the look of the development suggests. The overall density (number of dwellings divided by the total area) of a neo-traditional or eco-village development is often quite comparable to that of a conventional subdivision. With no savings on land, housing prices will not come down. Designer suburbs are not meant to be affordable.

In a way, the designer suburbs can be interpreted as an effort by the elite to reclaim the earlier suburban ideals of democracy and community, lost through the invasion of the masses. No where is this more clearly illustrated than in its conception and treatment of open space.

There is a shift from yards to parks, that is, from individual private open space to communal open space. This is aimed at catering to the life-cycle of the old and life-style of the young. There are fewer children and fewer parents who stay at home. The emphasis is on larger open spaces rather than "fragmented" ones - spaces that celebrate the community spirit and protect natural habitats. In fact, if designer suburbs catch on in a big way there may be significant regional consequences. We will have picturesque sprawl. Instead of Le Corbusier's "towers in the park" we will have "horizontal towers in a sea of green." There won't be much savings in land and infrastructure over the conventional suburban sprawl of old.

As environmental ideals, gentrified homes and luxury condominiums in the inner city raise different questions. Presently they are not very affordable. But can costs be reduced without compromising livability?

Gentrified tenements, mews, lofts and cottages have the latest and most advanced gadgets to make them very livable, or even enjoyable, for the small yuppie and empty-nester households. Retrofitting often costs more than building a new house.

The central issue, however, is "crowding." Of course, "dense" environments are not necessarily crowded: a neighbourhood of high-rise luxury apartments would have quite adequate living space for its residents. However, outside of the gentrified enclaves, existing neighbourhoods of rowhouses and low-rise apartments typically have neighbourhood densities greater than those of high-rise areas.

I have studied the livability of such neighbourhoods and one major finding was that residents in these areas consistently showed lower satisfaction about shelter and neighbourhood quality than those living in single-detached or high-rise areas. The greatest discrepancy between user expectation and satisfaction concerned privacy, perhaps the single most significant negative effect of crowding. It seemed that people here had greater problems deciding whether they expected anonymity or engagement from their housing situation.

Direct entry at ground level, assumed to be the most positive selling point of the medium-density dwelling types, especially when compared to the high-rise, was viewed by residents as preferable but not essential. They would rather have bigger rooms, more storage space and more daylight. Their perception about security from crime and traffic accidents was found to relate more to "address" and land-use characteristics than to dwelling types or neighbourhood densities.

It seems that people share stereotypes about the single-detached house, duplex, triplex, rowhouse, garden apartment, etc. - the number of storeys, floor space, site coverage and the amount of private outdoor space, as well as household sizes and their socio-economic characteristics. There are generally accepted norms and expectations about spatial behaviour and neighbourly relations.

"New urbanism" introduces a differ-

... perception about security from crime and traffic accidents was found to relate more to "address" and land-use characteristics than to dwelling types or neighbourhood densities.

ent set of assumptions about how dwellings should be designed, and how they should relate to one another and to the land and environment around them. More significantly, it suggests how people should live. It will be to our peril to see the "humble" building forms without seeing the intention of exclusivity and status behind them. It is the "unspoiled nature" on the outside and "modern comfort" on the inside that make "new urbanism" attractive to the elite.

The reality of the neo-traditional designer suburbs is that they probably consume as much land as the conventional subdivision. On the other hand, gentrified ghettos are not affordable to most people while other conventional medium-density dwelling types have significant livability problems.

It seems there is no "free lunch." If all things are equal, packing a larger number of dwellings within a given area will necessarily reduce privacy, sunlight and space for everyone. Better design and more money would help, but that also means the product will be less affordable.

The merit of "new urbanism" lies not so much in what it delivers to the elite, but in how it can influence the ordinary citizen. It is about options. If there are enough people interested in trying it out, maybe some form of it will become affordable and acceptable to the masses. The irony is, though, by that time the elite may wish to move on, and "new urbanism" may be condemned for some yet to be invented sins.

Constraints

Residential Intensification: The Wrong Planning Debate

Ray Simpson

Ray Simpson is a Partner with Hemson Consulting Ltd.

The issue of residential intensification was a subject of interest throughout the Ontario planning community during the mid-1980s. This interest developed primarily in response to very real concerns at the time about the lack of availability of affordable housing. Intensification subsequently became a key element of the 1989 Land Use Planning For Housing Policy Statement, which proposed conversion and infill to provide many additional affordable housing units. Most recently, interest in residential intensification has increased in response to environmental concerns where intensification is seen as a way of limiting the amount of undeveloped land needed for housing.

Intensification is not a new process. It has been occurring in urban centres throughout Canada for many decades. Intensification is essentially a new term for an old process whereby communities incrementally add to or alter the built environment to accommodate new uses that reflect changing social and economic realities. Residential intensification can be categorized into five types: conversion of existing units or buildings; infill; redevelopment; adaptive re-use; and suburban densification.

In Ontario intensification is currently promoted as a "Holy Grail" through which we can overcome many of the negative impacts of urbanization. Its proponents claim that, among other things, intensification will: preserve farmland, save large sums of investment in infrastructure, reduce automobile dependency, and improve urban design. Intensification has been put forward as part of the solution to these problems but its role in achieving them is not yet clearly defined or understood. There are many unanswered questions. For example: What are the benefits and costs of intensification? When all costs are considered, will intensified urban development actually produce housing that is more affordable? Or is intensification merely being used to justify other policy goals such as setting infrastructure priorities or discouraging the designation of new areas for development?

During the last three or four years of my involvement in land use planning in Ontario, I have become increasingly aware of the need for a balanced perspective on residential intensification and its role in planning Ontario's future. I have five concerns with the current intensification debate.

The Public Does not Share Planners' Desire to Live in Intensified Communities

Throughout Canada and indeed much of the western world there is a strong preference for housing that is ground related and has private outside space. The results of focus groups and marketing surveys clearly illustrate that this dream is still alive and strong in Canada. In fact, in spite of low income growth and the worst affordability crisis in recent memory, more people in the Greater Toronto Area and elsewhere are living in single detached units. Massive ratepayer opposition to proposals to increase housing density in any form continues to occur in most communities.

Even with single-detached housing there are concerns about the visual and functional quality of the streetscape when lot sizes are squeezed. If we are going to increase the demand for housing forms other than single detached homes, we will need to do a better job of providing "medium density" housing. The current rigidity of the municipal planning environment has resulted in a lack of alternatives to single detached homes. Developing a greater acceptance of "medium density" housing is clearly the best opportunity to densify new residential neighbourhoods.

The Amount of Housing Potential from Intensification is Vastly Overstated

The "supply side" receives most of the attention when we try to determine the potential for intensification. Even on this side of the intensification equation most of the analysis has been too narrowly focused on the availability of physical sites.

To deliver real intensification three other supply side factors must be addressed: property owners' willingness to participate; supportive planning policy; and the presence of adequate services. It is only in situations where all four factors are present that intensification may occur.

Availability of a Physical Site: All communities provide numerous opportunities for residential intensification. Virtually all single and semi-detached dwelling units have the physical potential for an accessory apartment. Also, most communities have numerous larger scale sites where intensification projects could occur. Lack of physical sites is not normally a constraint to intensification.

Owners Must Perceive an Economic Benefit: Understanding who will produce intensification is critical. Potential producers of new development through intensification include: homeowners, local business persons, and developers/builders. Each type of potential producers has a different perspective on why it would want to intensify and the benefit to be expected. Property ownership patterns are also important. Where the ownership pattern is highly fragmented, there are usually competing interests making land assembly a difficult task.

Planning Policy Must Be Supportive: Planning policies and regulations significantly influence opportunities for intensification. The evidence to date in Ontario is that planning policies that support intensification are extremely controversial among resident groups who feel the new policies will result in too much change in their neighbourhoods.

Excess Service Capacity Must Exist: Intensification has frequently been promoted as having the benefit of making better use of existing infrastructure. In many neighbourhoods there may indeed be under-utilized sewage, water, and transit capacity that could be tapped by increased housing density. However, it is the deficiency of community and social service facilities that is increasingly viewed by community groups as grounds to oppose intensification. The availability of parks and green space is a common yet particularly difficult issue to resolve.

Intensification is not a new process. It has been occurring in urban centres throughout Canda for many decades. Intensification is essentially a new term for an old process whereby communities incrementally add to or alter the built environment to accomodate new uses that reflect changing social and econonmic realities.

To deliver real intensification, three other supply side factors must be addressed: property owners' willingness to participate; supportive planning policy; and the presence of adequate services

Overcoming these concerns is becoming a major hurdle for proponents of residential intensification.

It is only when these four supply side factors are all present that intensification is likely to be successful. In work undertaken in several communities by my firm we have found that the number of occasions when all four factors coincide is small, despite a large supply of physically appropriate sites.

Intensification Will Need to Focus on More Than Just Residential Land Uses

If intensification is to achieve the goal of greatly reducing the amount of land required for new urban development, it must focus on more than just the space required for private residences. In a typical community in southern Ontario, private residential land represents only about one-third of a community's urban land. Public and community uses account for a greater share of the land area. There has not been enough acknowledgement of the need to lower standards and to reconsider issues such as the size of school sites, and road widths and setbacks, among many others. In our experience there is even a growing incidence of cases where standards have been raised. For example, especially in response to environmental concerns, stormwater management programs in new residential communities can require up to 10 per cent of the land area. Other communities have been planned so tightly that the rural areas beyond the community are being called upon to serve as the location for churches, alternatives schools and major sport facilities. This is a result that is surely not in keeping with the intent of intensification.

Intensification of employment has been virtually ignored. The majority of employment in our urban areas does not occur in large office complexes. In fact most employment is being accommodated on "employment lands" at relatively low densities. Planners have little understanding of why development in employment areas is occurring in its current form.

This is distressing since the physical characteristics of our employment areas are increasingly cited as a major constraint to reducing automobile dependency.

Land Use Planning is too Weak a Tool to Change the Strong Economic and Social Forces Against Intensification

There are institutional, social, and cultural factors favouring single detached housing in Canada. These include taxation policies that encourage Canadians to occupy the most expensive house they can afford, comparatively lower property taxes on single detached housing in many parts of the country, subsidies to seniors to make it easier for them to remain in their homes, policies to encourage home ownership such as mortgage insurance and allowing the use of Registered Retirement Savings Plan funds for a house purchase, and numerous others.

There is a very real limit to what amount of change in human behaviour can be accomplished through land use planning, especially with regard to something as fundamental as our shelter and living space. The tools available to land use planners further weaken our ability to effect change in the face of the economic and social factors that militate against such change.

There is a very real limit to what amount of change in human behaviour can be accomplished through land use planning, especially with regard to something as fundamental as our shelter and living space.

Intensification is not Without Significant Costs

We do not have a clear understanding of the costs of intensification. Among the possible effects of intensification are a tremendous upward pressure on the prices of existing single detached units (to the benefit of the present owners), an increase in demand for second homes in the countryside, and greater pressure on communities less able to manage growth. I am not sure if we are ready to deal with these costs and the many other unforeseeable impacts.

Conclusion

The focus on residential intensification is misdirecting the planning debate in Ontario. For many years, all types of land use plans have been written based upon population and employment densities that are just not being achieved. Planners continue to plan based upon their desires as to how people should live, work, and travel, not based upon how people are actually choosing to live, work, and travel. An over-reliance on intensification in land use plans for the next twenty-five years will continue this pattern of planning for what is not likely to occur.

The reality is that the majority of growth over the next thirty years is going to be accommodated at the periphery of existing urban areas. Planners in southern Ontario need to focus increasingly on building communities at the edge. If we do not recognize this we will most likely continue the pattern of incremental planning we have followed in the past, and thus ensure that the development of new communities will continue to fall short of their potential.

Residential intensification is an important way of thinking about the development of new areas and the redevelopment of existing areas. Intensification will not result in much of a reduction in the need for new land for urbanization and it is not the answer to everything that is wrong with housing today. It has occupied too high a profile in planning circles for too long and needs to be tempered with more thoughtful analysis and debate on how to create better new communities at the edge.

Legal and Financial Constraints Impede Intensification

Ron Kanter

Readers of *The Intensification Report* are aware of numerous policy studies extolling the virtues of intensification. Most recently the Sewell Commission on *New Planning for Ontario* recommended that:

- all communities be planned to minimize the consumption of land;
- in existing built up areas, intensification and mixed uses be encouraged by appropriate land-use designations and zoning;
- extensions to build up areas served by public sewage and water only be permitted if the extensions have a compact form and a mix of uses that efficiently use land, infrastructure, and public service facilities.

According to the preliminary results of a survey reported in the first issue of this publication, support for intensification is strong among many groups, including municipal staff and the provincial government. If intensification is such a good idea, and has such widespread support, why don't we see more of it in our cities and towns? Why do we have so many studies promoting residential intensification, and so few successful projects?

Part of the answer lies with the prolonged recession, which has lead to a reduction in housing starts of all kinds. Many ratepayers and local politicians oppose intensification in their neighbourhoods. But in my view, should not underestimate the impact of planning law expressed through official plans (OP) and zoning by-laws, and financial tools such as development charges and assessment practices in inhibiting intensification, within and adjacent to existing communities.

How Official Plans Inhibit Intensification

Residential intensification by definition involves development of a site at a density that is higher than that which previously existed or was designated. Take a look at the official plans in effect in Ontario today. Virtually every OP contains a provision requiring new residential development to be compatible with existing residential neighbourhoods. Opponents of residential intensification can and will use such clauses as legal ammunition in their battles in many residential neighbourhoods.

Only a few Ontario official plans are clearly supportive of intensification. Of

Ron Kanter is a lawyer who practices land use, environmental and municipal law with the firm Dale and Dingwall. While serving as an MPP from 1987-1990, he prepared *Options for a Greater Toronto area Greenlands Study* for the Province of Ontario.

particular note is a recent amendment to the regional official plan in Ottawa-Carleton, OPA 127, approved by the Minister of Municipal Affairs in July of 1992, which includes the following provisions:

• Council supports intensification of land use for residential purposes through conversion, rooming, boarding and lodging houses, accessory apartments, infill, redevelopment and a more efficient use of land in new development.

• Council requires municipalities in the urban areas to include policies in local official plans to ensure that, at a minimum, one third of all new housing is medium or high density housing, including townhouses, stacked townhouses and apartments.

Some area municipal official plans contain the usual clause ensuring that new residential development is generally compatible with adjacent existing development patterns but also define and permit medium density housing in most residential communities. For example, the Oakville official plan permits Medium Density I Housing defined as:

• multiple attached dwelling types such as street townhouses, block townhouses,
• duplexes, triplexes, quadraplexes, maisonettes, etc. at an average site density not exceeding 30 dwelling units per site hectare.

It could be argued that such official plans contain provisions regarding intensification which are inconsistent if not contradictory.

How Zoning By-laws Prevent Intensification

Zoning by-laws are another factor inhibiting residential intensification in many Ontario communities. Many municipal zoning by-laws permit only two forms of residential use, low density single family housing and high density multiple family apartments. Recently there has been increased interest in zoning by-laws that permit medium density forms of development, which are variously described as

stacked townhouses, multiple horizontal dwellings, multiple attached dwellings, high density low rise, sky-light apartments, garden apartments, or casitas.

However, By-laws permitting medium density development usually apply only on a site-specific basis. For example, Mississauga Zoning By-laws 1827 & 1828 permit the construction of nearly a thousand residential units at the intersection of Hurontario Street and Glenn Hawthorne Boulevard. Among the housing types permitted are sky-light apartments defined as:

a building or structure not exceeding 5 stories in height where each dwelling unit has an independent entrance either directly or through a common vestibule.

Richmond Hill Zoning By-law 356-86 permits the construction of 336 multiple dwellings, to a maximum height of 10 meters, with a maximum number of 56 multiple attached dwellings, which are defined as follows:

a separate building containing two or more dwellings which are horizontally and/or vertically attached which may be entered from an exterior yard or from an internal common space or an access balcony and in which 50 per cent or more of the dwelling units have direct access to a garden or roof terrace.

Other sites which are now zoned for high density high-rise may not permit medium density building forms such as stacked town houses without rezoning or minor variances to permit increased building coverage or reduced building setbacks. Many developers will consider residential intensification on sites which are appropriately zoned, but will not incur the expense and delay which accompanies a rezoning application.

Development Charges Ignore Intensification

A third factor inhibiting residential intensification is the method by which most municipalities in Ontario calculate development charges, formerly known as lot levies. Under the Development Charges Act, Ontario municipalities may require developers to pay for the off-site costs of growing-related services for various forms of development. The cost to the municipality of providing hard services such as water and sewers normally varies with the type and location of development. That is, it is cheaper to service a medium density project located adjacent to existing services than a lower density development situated farther from existing services.

Most municipalities impose higher development charges per unit on single family residences than on multiple family apartments. But development charge by-laws are generally silent on the intermediate density building forms characteristic of residential intensification. If municipalities impose the same per unit charges on medium density as on low density projects, then developers (or occupants, if these charges are passed on) will pay higher charges than appropriate. In June 1993, the Town of Richmond Hill decided to characterize the project permitted by By-law 356-86 the same as a multiple unit project for development charge purposes. This decision will save the developer thousands of dollars per unit.

Moreover, virtually all municipalities in Ontario impose the same development charges for all developments (average cost pricing) rather than varying them to reflect differing costs for different locations (marginal cost pricing). Where average cost pricing is used, there is no incentive to develop close to existing services because the developer does not benefit from reduced costs.

Assessment Practices and Intensification

According to the Assessment Act, all residential properties in Ontario are to be assessed on the basis of their market value, defined as the amount that a willing buyer would pay to a willing seller. In practice, particularly in the Metro Toronto area, the ratio of assessed value to market value for multi-family rental properties far exceeds the ratio or assessed value to market value for single family ownership properties. Multi-family condominium projects were originally

assessed at a higher rate constant with multi-family rate consistent with multi-family rental, but court decisions held that condominium units should be assessed on the same basis as other owner occupied residences.

To date, there has been little experience with the assessment of either condominium or rental projects of intermediate density. If such projects are assessed at the higher rate typical of high density rental development, they will be more costly to build and live in than single family accommodation of comparable value.

From Constraints to Incentives

Many policymakers have elaborated on the advantages of intensification. More developers, large and small, are demonstrating interest in developing and redeveloping land at higher than customary densities. Legal and financial constraints, as well as opposition from ratepayers and local politician, continue to stand in their way. What steps are required to move from constraints to incentives for intensification?

The Ministry of Municipal Affairs could enact model official plan and zoning by-law provisions to encourage more municipalities to permit residential intensification for a broad range of sites which they have already designated for residential development. As planners and lawyers are aware, standard provisions can have considerable influence on land use practice. Municipalities could revise their official plans to replace the compatibility test with that of no adverse impact. Residential intensification could also be encouraged by recognition and support in development charge by-laws. Assessment practices could be clarified to ensure that medium density projects, regardless of tenure, are treated fairly in comparison with single family homes of comparable value.

The Ministry of Municipal Affairs could enact model official plan and zoning by-law provisions to encourage more municipalities to permit residential intensification....

Main Streets Initiative Handicapped by Building Codes

Eberhard Zeidler

Eberhard Zeidler
is a Principal
with Zeildler
Roberts
Partnership
Architects.

It started as an idea whose time had come. Editorials were written about it. The Council embraced it. A competition was mounted to explore its architectural possibilities. The idea was to urbanize our underused main streets with five-storey *apartment buildings*, which would increase the number of people living in the city and create better use of the existing infrastructure. But today, some five years later, it has produced nothing more than several convoluted bylaws to be passed and woeful editorials about the future of the scheme.

It behooves us to explore the reasons for the fizzle of a great concept, as it may help us to learn for the future or even get this idea realized some day.

I do not think we can blame the failure to build according to the Main Streets concept on the current recession. This plan should have encouraged building in a time of recession, because it deals with small, affordable, and sustainable development, and would use the existing infrastructure economically. Why is it such a good idea to build additional density by going up to five-storey buildings along some main streets in Toronto?

Historically, the main streets of Toronto grew rapidly before the First World War and seemed to be formed by a never-ending line of prototypical structures, mainly two or three storeys in height, with retail along the street enlivened by pedestrians, and one or two-storey apartments or offices above. Much of Queen Street West, Spadina, St. Clair, and Eglinton are still this way, although they were interrupted by some large developments after the Second World War. These new developments were based on modern planning theory, which regarded buildings as isolated sculptures unfolding their individual functions to the optimum, and regarded the street not as a related pedestrian realm but as a two-dimensional vehicular traffic connection.

The life of the street as the realm of the pedestrian was rediscovered through the eyes of Jane Jacobs and others. To prevent further erosion of the street through new development, bylaws were designed to maintain the building stock along the main streets and restrict their height to three storeys. Since there was little economic advantage for individuals to build a new building on these lots without any gain in density, the buildings just stayed. They are, in fact, still the backdrop of some of the most delightful and culturally rich urban life in Toronto. Most exist in a mildly ecaying atmosphere but still provide room for urban commercial experiments.

I have watched the death and life of Queen Street East and West over the last 20 years from my office windows. The life that has slowly come back into that street demands respect and careful scrutiny.

European architects and planners who have visited me over these 20 years have been amazed when they see this urban scene. They admire the lively urban drama on these streets - people crowding them at all times of day and night, even all times of the year (astonishing in our climate). However, they are astonished too by the tawdry visual scene they see. In addition to the intrusive hydro poles and broken sidewalks are the collapsing facades of vintage buildings, occasionally broken by crude, modern box interventions or an beautifully restored Victorian facade. In their minds, they compare it unfavourably to the typical European street that was created at the turn of the century - from Haussmann's Paris boulevards to the streets of Berlin or Madrid. They were given their life support not only through retail but also through other activities in these 60- to 70-foot-high buildings, which presented not only a beautiful visual enclosure of the street but also an intricate mix of functions above the street-level commercial activities. Here are all kinds of office and living spaces. The living quarters, furthermore, were mixed in social status, from the upper classes who lived on the first and second floors, to the caretakers and bohemians who lived in the garrets.

It was the smoke-belching factories of the industrial revolution that caused laws with the power to destroy this urban paradigm. Modern planning theory believed the city had to be rescued by a segregation of functions. Work here. Housing there. Shopping here. Schools there. The result was urban sprawl and an unsustainable high cost and public debt for infrastructure.

In our postindustrial era we do not need the separation of work from living as seemed so necessary when noisy factories intruded. Today, offices can live easily beside apartments and stores. The typical European street with its social mix can become a model; it would involve changing the planning rules to permit five-storey apartment buildings along major Toronto streets such as St. Clair, Queen and the Danforth.

Housing on Main Streets would also bring work and living closer together, within easy walking distance of existing public transportation systems, thereby reducing pollution by diminishing the use of the car. It all sounded reasonable and achievable, and five years later one should have seen the first examples of this experiment. However, no real birth has taken place.

One can only ask why. Some have said that the inability to change cumbersome parking requirements is the main reason. However, I feel that another more important problem preventing the realization of the concept has been the lack of a Canadian housing prototype that could be used in the situation. The prototype used in Europe to realize such street development has a central street entrance that leads to a gracious stairway connecting five or six levels. On each level are two apartments for residential or office use. On the first level, along the main street, are mostly stores or cafes. However, on more residential streets (such as the side streets) one often finds that the

first level is a half-level above the street, with a janitor's apartment below. This first residential level is the most desirable, the so-called piano nobile.

You might ask why can't we do the same? Very simply, because our building bylaws do not allow us to have 10 or 12 apartment units exited by a single stair. Our bylaws demand that from each apartment we must reach a corridor from which two independent stairs exit. This appears to be a reasonable precaution for life safety. However, the life safety of this single-stair type in Europe has been equal to, if not better than ours. I still do not know why our codes could not provide for the European prototype, because it would allow us to build self-contined buildings along the main streets on relatively small lot widths. A lot as small as 50 feet could be used efficiently. With our current building laws, we require 200 feet or larger lots to build competitively, which usually requires land assembly.

The suggested one-stair prototype creates not only the advantage of "buildability" on relatively small lots but also low energy consumption. Each unit now opens to opposite sides, either south and north or east and west, and makes through-ventilation of each apartment possible. This means in our climate one could easily live in comfort almost without air conditioning, aside from a few sweltering days in the summer. The other urban advantage is these buildings can be built along east-west as well as north-south streets for, regardless of direction, each apartment would have sun exposure in addition to through-ventilation. The central corridor apartment building that our codes demand must preferably be placed in a north-south direction so each apartment has either east or west exposure and some sun. If we place such a building in an east-west direction, only the south apartments have sun; the north ones never see it. The result would be that one could build this type of housing not only along north-south streets but also along east-west streets such as St. Clair or Queen St.

I believe until we introduce building bylaws that allow for this single-stair prototype, we will not be able to build along the main streets in a sustainable way.

Sprawl and Intensification

Ken Whitwell

Ken Whitwell is currently Head of the Development Services Department for the City of York. He was previously an affiliate of the IBI Group in Toronto and Assistant Deputy Minister of Community Planning for the Province of Ontario. He has also served as Commissioner of Planning for the City of Scarborough, and was the Chief Planner of Policy and Research for the City of Toronto.

Planning in the Province of Ontario. He has also servied as Commissioner of Planning for the City of Scarborough, and as the Cheif Planner - Policy and Reaearch for the City of Toronto.

For many years, I, like many other planning professionals, have advocated a policy of intensification of development and the containment of sprawl. Lately, I have begun to question this position.

My concern is the absence of a public client group. Conceptually, in a free market system people make choices; in a democracy governments reflect those choices. The role of a professional is to provide advice and to explain the costs, benefits or other consequences of proposed actions. But people are quite free to choose a costly action if they perceive that the benefits outweigh the costs. Furthermore, if a position has no support group, particularly if there are powerful interests in opposition. It would be better to concentrate on attainable changes than to pursue theoretically thoughtful but politically futile policy goals.

Who are the groups affected by sprawl and what are their interests?

The Rural Area

Many people in the rural areas wish to preserve the family farm and the traditional rural way of life. Given the present state of the farm economy, the only way that many farmers can remain on the land and provide for their families is to sell parts of the farm land for new residential development. The creation of new building lots out of farm land not only provides housing for additional family members, but also a source of capital for required renovations and purchases.

Local rural township officials generally have a positive view of new residential development. The largest local expenditure for many councils is road maintenance. The addition of a few more cars does not significantly increase road costs but the additional taxes benefit their revenues.

Existing residents see the new population as providing more students to the local schools which otherwise might be closed and consolidated due to declining enrollments. Local businesses, churches, community and cultural groups, and service organizations also see increased population as a benefit in supporting their activities.

Thus any concerted effort to restrict sprawl by refusing further rural severances or sub-divisions and by directing all new development to existing urban areas would not be supported by a large segment of the rural population.

The New Suburbs

As the wealth of people increases, more living space is one of the benefits purchased. While there are obviously those who prefer a denser more downtown-type living style, for families with children, the dwelling unit of choice is the single family home. Any policy to curtail the size of residential lots must deal with this desire for more living space, as many people make a choice for larger homes and larger lots if they can afford to do so.

From the perspective of a municipal council, if land is sold per foot frontage or per acre, then the value of the land of a new subdivision with be the same regardless of the lot sizes. A 60 foot lot will cost twice as much as a 30 foot lot. Assuming there is a relationship between land costs and building costs. If the land is twice as expensive, the house built on it will be twice as expensive. Residential taxes reflect residential property values. Thus the municipality would collect twice as many tax dollars from a large house on a 60 foot lot as it would from a smaller house on a 30 foot lot. Municipal revenues are, therefore, roughly the same per acre regardless of lot size.

On the expenditure side, municipal

costs for roads and services are either the same or slightly less per acre with larger lots. However, people costs for such services as education, recreational facilities, welfare, etc are significantly reduced if the population is reduced. This then leads a prudent municipality, faced with a fixed land area, to develop that land with as few and as large houses as possible. Revenues are the same, but costs are lower with the larger lots and resulting fewer people.

In comparison, from the provincial perspective, government is faced with housing a fixed number of people. People related costs are the same regardless of where they live. However, infrastructure costs in total can be reduced if the population consumes less serviced urban land. Thus a prudent province attempts to reduce urban land consumption.

As long as local municipalities are making planning decisions, there is no great financial impetus for them to reduce densities and to provide for more intensified development. This is particularly so as their constituents favour large lots and houses and would be strongly opposed as attempts to curb lot sizes.

Urban Areas

People living in urban areas, having chosen a more urban life style could be expected to be the one group favouring intensification and a curtailment of sprawl.

In Toronto, the Yonge-Eglinton area has developed a reputation for fine restaurants, specialty stores, a varied nightlife and a vibrant pedestrian environment. This area, plus the developments at Yonge-St. Clair and at Davisville also provide the backbone of support for the Yonge subway and help to subsidize bus routes in lower density areas. The development around these subway stations is a classic example of transit supportive land use planning and urban intensification

The development, however, of the apartments at these locations was vigorously opposed by local residents at the time that they were being planned and built.

The opposition of city residents to intensification continues to this day. One of the few remaining objections to the recently adopted Toronto Official Plan is to the intensification policies of the Main Street program.

In fact, while city residents may give lip service to the notions of containing sprawl and encouraging intensified suburban development, they, like their suburban counterparts, resist any intensification in their own neighbourhoods.

Environmental Interests

One of the interest groups that one might suppose would be actively encouraging intensification would be the "environmentalists". However, frequently those who have the greatest interest in the preservation of natural areas are also those who favour lower densities to minimize impacts on adjacent natural areas and like large lots with ample vegetation, trees and open space.

I have never experienced the situation where people who support the protection of the natural environment have appeared before a municipal council arguing that the density of a proposed development was too low or that the lot sizes proposed were too large.

Regulators and Other Bureaucrats

The land takings of various public agencies in redevelopment projects are now about 50 per cent of the original land area. Land is required to expand the right-of-way of boundary streets; internally right-of-way requirements are now usually 24 to 30 metres; parkland is almost never just five per cent, school sites are larger and there is often an additional municipal requirement for a buffer or set-back from adjacent uses.

In new subdivisions, there are requirements for the preservation of woodlots, stream beds and other natural areas, over and above any required parkland. Municipal engineers require land to be dedicated for storm water detention ponds and overland flow routes. All of these dedications mean an increase in the total land requirements to accommodate a given number of people.

In fact, while city residents may give lip service to the notions of containing spawl and encouraging intensified suburban development, they, like their suburban counterparts, resist any intensification in their own neighbourhoods.

In addition to land takings, there are significant restrictions on the development of the remaining land. Planning regulations requiring on site parking, single use areas, minimum lot sizes, building setbacks, retention of obsolete industrial land, and a maximum number of dwelling units per acre result in increased sprawl and auto dependency. However, there does not appear to be any countervailing interest group espousing intensification. No group is pushing for smaller school sites or less parkland. Rate payer groups do not often mobilize in favour of increased densities. Thus political decisions, which usually are a compromise between competing interests, continue to discourage intensification and to result in a continuation of a sprawling metropolis.

Conclusions

The planning profession has long concluded that intensification and the avoidance of sprawl is a "good thing". By and large, however, this is a not a conclusion reached by most of the communities affected by sprawl. Rural areas will be concerned that intensification policies are simply an attempt by big cities to hog all of the growth and to relegate small towns and villages to stagnation and a slow death. Suburban areas will see intensification policies as an attempt to prohibit their attainment of a desired life style and to impose "affordable" housing, congestion and urban chaos into their communities. City people will see such policies as the victory of developers pushing high rise buildings and more people into their neighbourhoods, overloading the schools and parks, and producing parking and traffic chaos.

Only the provincial government has the perspective of saving money through reduced infrastructure investment which would result from higher densities. But the province must reflect the composite interests of the electorate and there is no consensus of opinion that the benefit of saving infrastructure dollars is greater than the perceived costs.

To Whom do Things Belong? The Limits of Intensification

Alan Waterhouse

Alan Waterhouse is a Professor of Planning, in the Department of Geography at the University of Toronto.

Successful inquiry begins, of course, by asking the right questions. Is this what those who advocate intensification have been doing? In a recent paper (Plan Canada 35.5, 1995), Pierre Filion described the increasingly dismal polarization of planning discourse and the hard facts of ongoing urban development. The planning community (and a few others) continue to weave their consensus on the virtues of reurbanization, while the centrifugal engine of metropolitan formation shows not the slightest sign of beginning to operate in reverse. The fiscal crisis, NIMBYism, a ten-year stockpile of approved low-density projects, and a stubborn refusal to give up the automobile - these things seem insurmountable.

Many advocates of intensification find it difficult to understand, let alone confront the events that spoil their aspirations, largely because of the questions they have been asking. The failure to ask the right questions, in this case, has led to a classic planning impasse, in which realistic limits have not been placed around policy expectations, while opportunities to pursue these expectations have gone unnoticed. This failure offends the first principle of pragmatism, whereby means and ends are necessarily intertwined from the beginning of any prescriptive exercise, so that objectives can be tempered by an awareness of what is immovable, and strategies realigned accordingly. Instead, the discourse on intensification has been monopolized by a single subordinate question: Where do things belong?

To ask where things belong leads straight into the philosophical cul-de-sac of spatial rationalism. Advocates of intensification, accordingly, deal at the level of end-state justification, pitching essentially similar accounts of the superior effects to be enjoyed from an intensified spatial order against the dire consequences of urban sprawl. They do so because of a well-entrenched (although hardly well-founded) belief, first, in the persuasive powers of end-state reasoning in the sphere of territorial politics; and secondly in a public interest that is both seamless and universal. According to this belief, intensification is good for everyone; we must simply put things where they belong.

To ask where things belong may seem to be the primordial planning question. What could be more fundamental than specifying the geography of human activity? But, as Donald Krueckeberg asks in "The Difficult Character of Property" (*Journal of the American Planning Association* 61.3. 1995), a better (and older) one would be "To whom do things belong?" Asking where things belong not only presupposes the eventual emergence of a public consensus on the answer, it also covers the root and manifestations of the conflict accompanying any attempt to meddle with property. Any disclosure on the effects of sprawl needs to be nuanced by first dealing with causes, and causes only be revealed by developing a thorough - and sympathetic - understanding of the role that property plays in the psyche and everyday life of those affected by the intensification vision.

Planning history overflows with diatribes against property ownership as the mother of all sins. The caricatured landlord, in fact, still performs the dragon role in many a campaign to establish the new spatial order. But because hardly anyone still believes in a 'natural' right to unrestrained liberal ownership, the caricature is outmoded, and was always misleading. Property ownership, and property rights, are far more complicated than the caricature suggests. John Christman, for instance, in *The Myth of Property: Towards an Egalitarian Theory of Ownership* (New York: Oxford University Press, 1994) identifies nine distinct kinds of property rights: possession, use,

alienation, consumption, modification, destruction, management, exchange, and profit taking. All these shades of 'ownership' affect the spatial order, and any propensity to divide property merely into public and private categories never comes close to the layered, overlapped, partial, and multiple character of property rights. Krueckeberg shows, for instance, how possession and use (but not the remaining categories) are linked, in our society, to deeply-rooted instincts associated with the expression of the self. In the absence of alternative means of self-expression in the spheres of work and community, the possession and use of property assume the greatest importance in everyday life, extending far beyond the boundaries of proprietorship. To 'possess' property, in these circumstances, is to 'possess' (in a different, but no less important sense) a claim on one's neighbour's property, a claim that is reciprocated and shaped by social norms governing everyday public behaviour. This claim, the ancestor of externality zoning, underlies the constructed relationships we call urban form, especially in the residential setting. It accounts, on the one hand, for great diversity of these forms, and on the other hand, for their underlying sameness and historical durability. We experiment with them at our peril because the forms are manifestations - effects - of a cause that resides, not in some putative dialectic of public and private interests, but in something rather more complicated and fundamental. To usurp the claim to one's neighbour's property, in short, is to damage the expression of oneself. In regarding NIMBYism as reactionary, selfish, and xenophobic we seriously underestimate its stubborn power and historical purchase.

Give the multiple shades of property interests, the equivalence given in law to corporate and individual property rights remains a paradox. The corporation, by and large, exhibits few effects of the link between possession and self-expression. Consumption, modification, management, and profit-taking can occur without a trace of psychic investment in property, so corporate vulnerability is of a different order from that of the individual in a

In the absence of alternative means of self-expression in the spheres of work and community, the possession and use of property assume the greatest importance in everyday life, extending far beyond the boundaries of proprietorship.

residential setting. Similarly, the attachment to one's place of work, even if proprietary rights include actual possession, are invariably weaker than the attachment to home. Consequently, the intensity of the workplace might be subjected to experiment provided that the particular rights to property characterizing non-residential locations remain secure. In this regard, two immediate issues need to be addressed. First, the undoubted attractions of mixed land uses are diminished to the extent that the question To Whom Do Things Belong? reveals unacceptable, or unadaptable patterns of property rights. Secondly, highly disparate intensities between the residential and remaining locations do little to reduce the incidence of automobility.

Of greater long-term concern, however, is our meagre understanding of property relations in the productive and retail sectors, and of the consequences of altering these relations by, say, staking a claim for greater public modification rights. Solid empirical work on the links between intensity and productive efficiency hardly exists; nor do we know much about ongoing shifts in commercial and industrial intensity, especially in suburban locations, yet their aggregate effect must be profound. At issue is the right to profit-taking from property use (not necessarily possession), especially the extent to which the ability of large-scale productive interests to accumulate capital is threatened by any plan, given their potential clout and footloose potential. The owners of suburban and exurban manufacturing, in this respect, present an especially hard case. Automobile-dependent shiftwork remains a stubborn obstacle to efficient transit operations, and truck-dependency is so entrenched that any demands for internal adaptation to higher intensities would be nothing short of punitive. Moreover, because manufacturing location users and profit-makers rely almost entirely on private transportation, the intensity of origin, as well as destruction locations, will probably remain low.

Regulated shifts to high intensity necessarily entail reductions in the supply of serviced land; indeed, such reductions form one of the primary objectives of

reurbanization. The consequent upward pressure on services and land rent favours one group of owners at the expense of others. As a factor of production and retailing to adapt internally under conditions of intensification. But we know virtually nothing about the subject. What we do know, from a few studies of the highly regulated retail sector in Germany, for instance, suggests that policies of urban containment do inflate the price of consumer goods. If this same picture also characterizes the production sector, then the winners, as in the nineteenth century city, are certain landowners. Everyone else, particularly those who possess few or no property rights at all, lose. Again, asking To Whom do Things Belong? exposes the fallout from, and potential opposition to the grand vision.

The same question refocusses attention too on the overlapping spheres of public and private rights to property, and in so doing reveals that the two are not only competitive, but also reciprocal and complementary. Infrastructure provision, even regulation, are not the exclusive preserve of government, any more than the market can lay sole claims to the provision of private goods. The ownership of density rights, for instance, gets complicated by the historic relationship between private affluence and the propensity to consumer space, especially residential space. This propensity is augmented by government programs that inordinately underwrite the servicing of low density locations. As Igor Vojnovic has recently pointed out (*Intensification Report*, 1994), the private possession of (low) density rights comes at a high public cost; expressed differently, the possession of low density rights necessarily entails high consumption rights in public goods. But the chances for intensification must wait until fiscal politics takes this wider view of ownership and obligation into account.

Does any good news emerge from asking who owns what? Because the question is rarely asked, it would be difficult to know. A much-touted model in the intensification campaign is the "successful" European City, fine-grained, compact, highly regulated, regionally governed. The spatial morphology and

If this same picture also characterizes the production sector, then the winners, as in the nineteenth century city, are certain landowners. Everyone else, particularly those who possess few or no property rights at all, lose. Again, asking To Whom do Things Belong? exposes the fallout from, and potential opposition to the grand vision.

activity patterns of these places are well understood. But to whom do things belong? To what extent does the incidence of leaseholds and tenancy, or of small-scale ownership of production, commerce, and retailing play a part? Are means of self-expression other than proprietorship well-developed? Does internal adaptation to high intensity affect the price of real estate, services, and of capital and consumers goods? To what extent does the affluence of owners affect the consumption of space? Because so much is at stake in the intensity campaign, these, and questions like them, need to be asked.

Suburban Intensification in the GTA

Ray Tomalty

Because the benefits of intensification are often regional in nature, while the costs are local and site-specific, intensification is usually promoted by provincial governments and often resisted by local governments. This study uses a case study approach to explore the interplay between provincial and municipal interests in a particular region. The subject region is the Greater Toronto Area, where the conflict between provincial and local interests is especially fierce in suburban regions because:

- land is still available for greenfield development and developers are a powerful influence on local growth politics;
- the types of land use patterns that the province wants to address through intensification are especially evident i.e., exclusive, auto-based, low-density neighbourhoods; and,
- the vast majority of the population and employment growth over the next 30 years is expected to occur in suburban areas.

Recent official planning activity in suburban areas of the Greater Toronto Area (GTA) provide rich material for studying planning policy and the interaction of planning authority in the region: over the last five years, all of the upper-tier municipalities and over half the lower-tier municipalities have issued new plans or have been engaged in major official plan amendments. For these reasons, it was decided to focus the research on suburban areas. The principle questions being asked are:

- What is the provincial policy framework to encourage intensification at the local and regional levels?
- How are suburban municipalities at both levels of government responding to policy pressures from the provincial government and the changing planning context favouring intensification?
- How can that response be explained?

The first question is answered by reviewing provincial policy documents. The second is addressed by a review of official plans of the four upper-tier suburban municipalities. Addressing the third question involves interpreting the official plan findings using in-depth interviews conducted with 80 provincial planners, and the use of supporting planning documents.

It helps to analyze intensification policy efforts into three categories: growth management, housing intensification, and urban structure policies. I will report very briefly on the finding in each category.

Growth Management
The province's growth management objectives are expressed in the following key documents:

- The 1991 Growth and Settlement

Ray Tomalty is a Ph.D. candidate at the University of Waterloo. This article is from a report on research that was supported by the federal Tri-Council, Canada Mortgage and Housing Corporation and ICURR, the Intergovernmental Committee on Urban and Regional Research.

Guidelines, incorporated into the Planning Reform package of 1995. They promote compact, contiguous development that minimizes fiscal and environmental impacts.

• The regional distribution of population on the 1993 study entitled Outlook for Population and Employment in the GTA, prepared for the Office of the Greater Toronto Area. The study projected population distributions amoung the GTA's five upper-tier municipalities according to a Reference

Population targets:

The table below gives some information about population projections in the region. The OGTA's Reference Scenario and Intensification Scenario are shown along with the numbers appearing in the regional official plans. The key figures are in the final column, indicating whether the regional official plans have met the OGTA population targets for the Intensification Scenario. The table shows that only two of the four upper-tier plans have incorporated the OGTA targets.

Comparison of GTA Population Targets

	Year	OGTA Reference	OGTA Scenario 1	ROP	ROP - Scenario 1
Metro	2011	2.387	2.541	2.500	-0.041
Peel	2021	1.324	1.255	1.328	+0.073
York	2021	1.287	1.107	1.100	-0.007
Durham	2021	0.969	.952	0.970	+0.018
Halton	2011	0.547	0.534	0.530	-0.004

Scenario based on the successful implementation of current intensification policies. This scenario showed that about 95 per cent of new growth going to suburban regions. A more aggressive intensification scenario was also projected based on more growth being redirected to Metro Toronto, away from the suburban regions. Known as Scenario 1, it was the growth option selected by the provincial government for incorporation into upper-tier regional plans.

The key mechanism for expressing the provincial objectives is through the upper-tier regional plans. In approving the upper-tier plans, the Ministry of Municipal Affair's planning approvals branch set a series of "land budgeting" goals based on the policy framework:

• incorporate the OGTA population objectives into the regional official plans;
• increased densities for greenfield development; and,
• increase the proportion of new population accommodated through intensification as opposed to green field development.

Deviations are significant in two cases, Peel and Durham, where the population projections incorporated into official planning documents are higher than the OGTA targets. In both cases, the official plan projects a number actually slightly in excess of the OGTA Reference Scenario, which was based on past development trends in the GTA. In York Region, the population figure is currently under criticism from a number of area municipalities that would like to see their targets increased. If all increases are given, and there is a distinct possibility of this, it would raise the York number approximately halfway to the Reference Forecast from its current level. This would leave only Halton with a plan that substantively reflects the OGTA population targets.

Minimum Densities

The Ministry's objective was to have regional official plans incorporated minimum density objectives for all new development, applied on a region-wide basis. A level of 10 upa (units per acre) gross density was initially considered in negotiations with

Durham but the goal was eventually reduced to 7 upa.

Provincial planners were unsuccessful in convincing regional officials to formally incorporate minimum densities in their Official Plans. None of the plans incorporated clearly stated minimum densities to be achieved in new developments. Halton, however, is preparing an Urban Structure Plan, which will eventually become part of the official plan through the official plan amending process. The draft plan proposes an average gross density of about 8 upa.

In two other cases, minimum densities were incorporated into official plans in more subtle, if less enforceable, ways. In Durham's case, the regional official plan (ROP) states as one of the four bases of the plan that "over time, the density of new development will continue to increase" but does not assign any numerical targets. According to regional staff, however, a target of 7 upa is considered to be a "background assumption" of the plan and will be used when considering lower-tier municipal plans, plan amendments and plans of subdivisions.

In York Region, density targets are also subtly expressed. Rather than explicitly stating any minimum densities in the official plan, they are implied by a "sidebar illustration" in the plan. The sidebars suggests that a typical new community would have a gross density of about 6 upa. Because this is not a formal goal stated in the plan, however, it is not considered an official target.

In Peel Region, target densities for new development are not expressed in the draft plan, but there is planning assumption that densities will be in the order of 9 ups, including residential lots and the internal road pattern, but excluding parks, schools and major arterials. Once these land uses are included, the resulting densities would be about 6 upa.

Although these density targets may represent a significant change from conventional development patterns in suburban areas, several caveats are in order. First, the densities are not higher than those being developed through the action of market forces in some suburban areas in the GTA. Secondly, the definition of density called gross density used by the Ministry of Municipal Affairs in its approval deliberations excludes the land protected by the variety of provincial policies. This means that even if the pressures on regional officials to achieve higher gross densities were effective, what are sometimes called the super-gross densities, including environmental take-outs, may remain roughly constant or even be reduced.

Intensification targets

More successful from the provincial perspective has been its attempt to get regional official plans to incorporate intensification objectives, although here too, success is highly qualified. The Ministry's goal was for each regional plan to contain policies that would direct a minimum of 20 per cent of new growth to be achieved through intensification. Thus, designation of new land for development would be sufficient to accommodate a maximum of 80 per cent of the expected population growth of the region.

In two cases, a 20 per cent intensification objective is included in the plan and land budgets were adjusted accordingly. The Durham Official Plan, for instance, states "Intensification is encouraged within existing urban areas. Further, as an overall target, the Region, in conjunction with the area municipalities, will plan to accommodate approximately 20 per cent of all new population growth through intensification."

The 20 per cent intensification target has also been expressed in the official plan for the Region of York. Halton's plan implies an intensification objective of over half of new development. In Peel, the draft official plan does not include any intensification objectives, although this plan is in the draft stage and this may be a matter of discussion between the Ministry of Municipal Affairs and the Peel planning team.

Although the 20 percent intensification target was met or superseded in three of the four plans, it is important to realize that the meaning of intensification for this purpose is not clear. An analysis

None of the plans incorporated clearly stated minimum densities to be achieved in new development.

of the working definition (which has yet to be finalized and agreed to by area municipalities, the province and regional council) being developed in Durham shows that intensification claims are clearly inflated. Intensification, according to this definition, refers to development on land that was "built up" as of June 5, 1991, the date of the adoption of the Durham official plan. The meaning of "built up" here is critical: it refers to any land that had any structure on it at the time even if it were a single house on 10 acres of land. It also included lands on which there were registered plans of subdivision but excluded those with only draft approval. The boundaries were drawn using this definition and aerial photos for guidance.

Using this definition, the boundary of the "built up area" is more or less coterminus with the urban boundary appearing in previous regional plans. Thus, greenfield development at any density will be counted as "intensification" as long as it occurs within the previously existing boundary. There is no reason to doubt that this will become the standard for judging the 20 per cent intensification goal adopted by Durham, York and Halton. In the Halton Region, approximately 54 per cent of new growth will be accommodated within the urban boundary established in the 1980 official plan, but this includes 38 per cent to be accommodated on vacant land and only 16 per cent in the already built up area. Thus, the intensification target for this region using the conventional definition of the word is only 16 per cent. This figure is probably above existing trends, but it is difficult to judge the magnitude of the difference.

Housing Intensification Policies
Detailed comparison of provincial policy objectives with municipal plans has also been carried on for housing intensification policies. The province's policy objectives are expressed in the *Housing Policy Statement for Land Use Planning* (1989) and the Residents Rights Act (1994). A comparison of the provincial objectives with the policies contained in lower-tier municipal plans shows that lower-tier municipalities in the region

have attempted to preserve municipal autonomy and power to control housing and development in the face of provincial policy intervention in this field. To do this, municipalities have adopted a number of strategies to reduce the planning impact of the provincial policy objectives, especially those relating directly to intensification policies. These strategies include:

• avoid designating existing neighbourhoods for different forms of intensification based on provincial policy requirements. Instead, plans tend to direct intensification pressures to the edges of neighbourhoods, along arterials, and in emerging nodes or centres of higher-density, mixed use development (see urban structure section below).

• comply with provincial policy objectives when political risks in doing so are low, such as with the requirement to supply serviced land or monitor housing conditions.

• adopt firm statements supporting provincial objectives in the preface to official plans, but only vague language in the legal text.

• openly challenge provincial policy objectives when the political risks of compliance are high, e.g., legalization of secondary suites. Confrontation between the municipality and the province allows the municipality to demonstrate where the political responsibility for the policy lies.

• cooperate with rather than try to control market forces. Most plans were found to contain intensification policies and objectives that were consistent with current market forces and showed little willingness to go beyond market trends.

Urban Structure Policies
The final stage of the research involves an examination of the emerging urban structure vision that is embodied in upper- and lower-tier plans in the GTA. This is compared to the provincial policy objectives as expressed in:

• the 1991 Transit Supportive Land Use Guidelines laying out general

Although the 20 per cent intensification target was met or superseded in three of the four plans, it is important to realize that the meaning of intensification for this purpose is not clear.

principles of urban structure based on a hierarchy of nodes and corridors

• the 1990 IBI report for the Greater Toronto Co-ordinating Committee called The GTA Urban Structures Concept Study;

• the specific regional structure suggested by the OGTA Working Group on Urban Form in its 1992 report. The group produced a map of the region showing where regional nodes would be located along with major corridors.

If one combines the four suburban regional urban structure plans and compares the result to the provincial visions, we find that the two differ in several respects. First, we note that the OGTA plan has 15 suburban nodes, two major (Mississauga and Oshawa) and 13 intermediate. The combined official plan version has 2.5 times that number: 33 nodes including Mississauga Square One and Oshawa.

In terms of the geographic location of the nodes, it is difficult to compare given the extreme generality of the OGTA urban structure plan and the dearth of references points by which to "pin down" the suggested positions. It appears, however, that of the 15 suburban nodes suggested by the OGTA work group, 11 are represented in the regional official plans by nodes in the approximate locations suggested by the OGTA. This implies that of the 33 suburban nodes on the combined official plan version, two-thirds or 22 are in locations not projected in the OGTA plan.

Unfortunately, given the lack of reference points in the official plans with respect to the anticipated size of the nodes, it is difficult to comment on this aspect of the proposed urban structure. York's plan, however, gives us a clue. It estimates that regional nodes would be in the order of 20-30,000 employees and 5-10,000 residents at a gross density of 4-6,000 residential and employees per hectare. This suggests a nodal land area of about 67 hectares. This figure is quite in line with that suggested in the OGTA report (i.e., up to 75 hectares for an

intermediate node).

The York plan also lets us assess the issue of the ratio of residents to employees. Taken the high number from the guideline of 5-10,000 residential to 20-30,000 employees in a node, the ration is one resident to three employees per hectare. This suggests a nodal land area of about 67 hectares. This figure is quite in line with that suggested in the OGTA report, i.e., up to 75 hectares for an intermediate node.

The OGTA urban structure map identifies a series of corridors linking the suburban nodes both along the Lake Ontario shore and in a half circle on the outside perimeter of Metro Toronto. The York plan designates a corridor along Highway 7 that would appear to coincide with the northern link of the half-circle. It also designates a length of Yonge Street that roughly corresponds to the OGTA plan, although the latter terminates in Richmond Hill while the York plan shows the corridor, after a little interruption, continuing on to Newmarket. Outside of the York Regional plan, however, no regional plan designated corridors. This, most of the corridor concept expressed in the OGTA report remains unrealized at the upper-tier official plan level.

Conclusion

Clearly, the provincial policy objectives on intensification are unevenly reflected in municipal plans in the GTA. Municipal planning has undergone significant changes in response to the changing provincial policy environment: more attention is paid to managing growth in a fiscally and environmentally sound manner, municipalities give more consideration to housing goals in their planning decisions, and there are signs that a loose urban structure is emerging through the official planning process. However, the analysis presented here clearly indicates that there are serious limitations on the ability of provincial policies to influence land use planning at the local level. By way of conclusion, we can do no more here than to mention some of the factors that may be involved:

Clearly, the provincial policy objectives on intensification are unevenly reflected in municipal plans in the GTA.

.... the analysis presented here clearly indicates that there are serious limitations on the ability of provicial policies to influence land use planning at the local level.

Provincial Policy Making

- decline of provincial leverage over municipal planning because of fiscal crisis;
- increasing municipal concern with local autonomy;
- public confidence in government in general and the planning system in particular has declined;
- no provincial agency that adequately "internalizes" the costs associated with urban growth;
- weak provincial policy instruments such as provincial policy statements and guidelines; and
- no consensus on definitions (e.g., no clear definition of what constitutes intensification and competing definitions of density).

Regional Planning

- poor co-ordination of provincial agencies at GTA-wide scale;
- suburban regions oppose concentrating growth in Metro;
- Metro municipalities oppose higher growth targets;
- lack of widespread awareness of regional issues/regional identity; and
- fragmentation of land use planning across 35 municipalities in the GTA.

Municipal Planning

- resistance to provincial policies;
- pressures from developers and property owners to designate more land for green-field development;
- planning constraints on redevelopment and infill development;
- servicing constraints on redevelopment and infill development (sewage, water, transit, road capacity, schools, etc.);
- political constraints on redevelopment and infill development;
- municipal councillors' accede to desire of residents and developers for lower density development;
- consumer preference for low-density, large-lot housing;
- resistance to higher densities from developers and property owners; and,
- resistance to higher densities from conservation groups.

Bibliography & Suggested Readings

Adams, R.E. "Is Happiness a Home in the Suburbs: The Influence of Urban Versus Suburban Neighbourhoods on Psychological Health", *Journal of Community Psychology*. 20 (4): 353-372.

American Farmland Trust. *Density-Related Public Costs*. 1986.

Aurora, Planning Department. *Housing Intensification: A Public Summary*. 1991.

Aurora, Planning Department. *Intensification: A Discussion Paper*. 1992.

Austin, Richard. *Adaptive Reuse: Case Studies in Building Preservation*. New York: Rheinhold Co. 1988.

Baird / Sampson, Urban Design Inc. *City of Toronto: Housing on Main Streets Economic Feasibility Study*, for the City of Toronto, Metropolitan Toronto & the Province of Ontario, June, 1990.

Barnett, Jonathan. *The Fractured Metropolis: Improving the New City, Restoring the Old City, Reshaping the Region*. New York: HarperCollins. 1995.

Bealer, B. and D.L. Poston. "Non-metropolitan America in Transition," *Rural Sociology*. 47 711-720, 1992.

Beaumont, Constance. *How Superstore Sprawl Can Harm Communities*, for National Trust for Historic Preservation. 1994.

Beckett, M.J. "Land Contamination" in Thomas Cairney (ed.) *Contaminated Land: Problems and Solutions*. London: Chapman and Hall. 1993.

Berridge, Lewinberg, Greenberg, Ltd. for the Municipality of Metropolitan Toronto, *Guidelines for the Reurbanization of Metropolitan Toronto*. December, 1991.

Brethour Research Associates Ltd. *Summary Report Market Study of Alternative Development Standards*. 1992.

Brown and Storey Architects & Michael Spaziani Architect. *Housing on Main Streets Demonstration Project Feasibility Study*: 1549 Danforth Avenue. 1992.

Brown, Donald A. "Recognizing the Limits of Risk Assessment," *Environmental Professional*, Vol. 14, p.185. 1992.

Brown, Lester and Jodi Jacobson. *The Future of Urbanization. Worldwatch Paper no. 77*. Washington D.C.: Worldwatch Institute. 1987.

Bryant, Christopher and Daniel Lemire. *Population Distribution and Management of Urban Growth in Six Selected Urban Regions in Canada*. 1993.

Button, K. and D. Pearce. "Improving the Urban Environment: How to Adjust National and Local Government Policy for Sustainable Urban Growth," *Progress in Planning*. pp. 137-184. 19__.

Calthorpe, Peter. *The Next American Metropolis: Ecology, Community and the American Dream*. New York, N.Y.: Princeton Architectural Press. 1993.

Campsie, Philippa. *The Social Consequences of Planning Talk: A Case Study on Urban Intensification*, Research Paper 190, Centre for Urban and Community Studies, University of Toronto, March 1995.

Canada Mortgage & Housing Corporation CMHC. *Healthy Housing Design Competition, Guide and Technical Requirements*. 1991.

Canada Mortgage & Houding Corporation. (CMHC) "Accessory Apartments: Characteristics, Issues and Opportunities", *Research Development Highlights*. NHA 6408, Issue 3, October 1991.

Canada Mortgage & Housing Corporation. (CMHC): Centre for Future Studies in Housing and Living Environments. *Reconsidering the Dream: Towards a Morphology for Mixed Density Block Structure in Suburbia*. 1992.

Canada Mortgage & Houding Corporation. (CMHC): Public Affairs Centre. *The Housing Industry: Perspective and Prospective. Summary Report, The Changing Housing Industry in Canada,* 1946-2001. 1988.

Canadian Council of Ministers of the Environment (CCME). *National Guidelines for Decommissioning Sites.* 1991.

Canadian Urban Institute (CUI), *A Guide to Creating a Historical Land Use Inventory of Potentially Contaminated Sites for Municipalities in Ontario.* 1994.

Canadian Urban Institute (CUI), *Housing Intensification: Policies, Constraints and Options,* 1991.

Canadian Urban Institute (CUI), *Lessons From Other Places: Planning the Toronto Region,* for the Office of the Greater Toronto Area, 1991.

Canadian Urban Institute (CUI). *The Case for Multifamily Housing.* 1991.

Capital Regional District. *Demand Capacity Land Use Analysis: Population, Housing and Employment in the Capital Regional District,* 1991-2001. 1993.

Caulfield, Jon. *City Form and Everyday Life: Toronto's Gentrification and Critical Social Practice.* Toronto: University of Toronto Press. 1994.

Center for Urban Studies (PSU) and Regional Financial Advisors, Inc. DLCD's *Local Government Infrastructure Funding in Oregon.* 1990.

Dauncey, Guy. "Eco-Community Design", *In Context, No.35.*

Demb, Alan. "Metro: Beyond Intensification, Reurbanization", *Toronto Planning Digest,* March, Vol. 6, No. 3, 1992.

Diamond, A.J. and Donald Schmitt and Company Architects and Planners. *City of Burlington Intensification Study: Public Participation Program Report.* 1991.

Diamond, A.J. and Donald Schmitt and Company Architects and Planners. *City of Burlington Intensification Study: Design Guideline Considerations Report.* 1991.

Dovers, Stephen. "Sustainability in Context: An Australian Perspective," *Environmental Management* 14(3), pp.297-305. 1990.

Downs, Anthony. *The need for a New Vision for the Development of Large U.S. Metropolitan Areas.* 1989.

Energy, Ministry of (MOEE). *Residential Energy Trends.* 1990.

Environment and Energy, Ministry of (MOEE). *Proposed Guidelines for the Clean-up of Contaminated Sites in Ontario.* PIBS 3161. 1994.

Environment Canada. *Economic Instruments for Environmental Protection.* 1992.

Flink, James J.. *The Automobile Age.* Cambridge, Mass.: MIT Press. 1990.

Fowler, E.P. "Land Use in the Ecologically Sensible City," *Alternatives* Vol.18, No.1 pp. 26-35, 1991.

Fowler, E.P. *Building Cities that Work.* Montreal: McGill Queen's University Press. 1992.

Frank, James E. *The Costs of Alternative Development Patterns.* 1989.

Friedman, A. and Vince Cammalleri. *Evaluation of Affordable Housing Projects Based on the Grow Home Concept.* Montreal: McGill University School of Architecture, Affordable Homes Program. 1992.

Frisken, Francis (ed.). *The Changing Canadian Metropolis: A Public Policy Perspective, Volume I & II,* Institute of Governmental Studies Press, University of California, Berkley and the Canadian Urban Institute. 1994.

Frisken, Francis. *Relating Municipal Land Use Practices to Public Transit Operations in the Greater Toronto Area: Constraints and Opportunities,* Ministry of Transportation, 1989.

Gardiner, Richard A. *Design for Safe Neighbourhoods.* National Institute of Law Enforcement and Criminal Justice. Sept. 1978.

Gaudet, C., A.Brady, M. Bonnel and M. Wong. "Canadian Approach to Establishing Clean-up Levels for Contaminated Sites," in *Petroleum Contaminated Soils and Ground-*

water, Vol.2. E.J. Calabrese and P.T. Kostecki (eds.). Proceedings from the First Annual West Coast Conference on Hydrocarbon Contaminated Soils and Groundwater. Lewis Publishers, Boca Raton, Florida. 1991.

Gilbert, Richard. *Cities and Global Warming.* Toronto: CUI. 1991.

Gordon, David. *Green Cities.* Montreal: Black Rose Books. 1990.

Greater Vancouver Regional District. *Liveable Region Strategy: Plan.* 1994.

Greenbelt Alliance, Bank of America, California Resources Agency and the Low Income Housing Fund. *Beyond Sprawl: New Patterns for Growth to Fit the New California.* 1995.

Hemson Consulting and Coopers & Lybrand Consulting Group. *The Outlook for Population and Employment in the GTA.* 1993.

Hemson Consulting, Halton Region Planning Department, Town of Milton Planning Department, Warren Sorensen Associates Inc., Gore & Storrie Ltd., Agplan Ltd., Robin Dee Associates, International Water Supply, McCormick Rankin, Ecoplan Ltd., Baird/Sampson Architects, C.N. Background Report 3-2: *Housing Intensification Opportunities in Urban Milton.* 1993.

Hemson Consulting, the Proctor & Redfern Group, Baird/Sampson Architects. *City of Guelph Housing Intensification Study.* 1992.

Hodge, Gerald. Canada's Aging Population: *The Role and Response of Local Government.* 1993.

Holliday, John. *City Centre Redevelopment.* New York: John Wiley & Sons Inc. 1973.

Hough, Michael. *City Form and Natural Process*: Towards a New Urban Vernacular, Routledge, London and New York, 1989.

House of Commons Environment Committee. *Shopping Centers and Their Future.* 1994.

Housing and Ministry of Municipal Affairs, Ministry of. *Making Choices: Alternative Development Standards Guidelines.* 1994.

Housing, Ministry of (MMA&H). *How to Create an Accessory Apartment.* 1990.

Institute of Traffic Engineers. *Traffic Engineering for Neo-Traditional Neighbourhood Design,* Technical Committee 5P-8. 1994.

Irwin, Neal. *A New Vision for Urban Transportation: Current Canadian Initiatives*, presented at the FCM/TAC/CIP Symposium "New Visions in Urban Transportation". 1994.

Isen, Engin & Ray Tomalty. *Resettling Cities, Canadian Residential Intensification Initiatives;* Main Report for CMHC, Ottawa, 1993.

Isin, Engin (ed.). *Toronto Region in the World Economy,* York University. 1994.

Isin, Engin and Ray Tomalty. *Resettling Cities: Intensification in Canada.* 1994.

J.L. Cox Planning Consultants. *City of North York Municipal Housing Needs Study: Volume I.* 1991

Jacobs, Jane. *The Death and Life of Great American Cities.* Toronto: Random House. 1961.

Kaplan, S. and R. Kaplan (eds.). *Humanscape: Environment for People.* Ann Arbor, Michigan: Urlich's Books Inc. 1982.

Katz, Peter. *The New Urbanism: Toward an Architecture of Community,* New York: McGraw-Hill. 1994.

Kidney, Walter. *Working Places: The Adaptive Use of Industrial Buildings.* Pittsburgh: Ober Park Associates. 1976.

Leung, Hok-Lin. Queen's University. *Residential Density and Quality of Life.* 1993.

Lynch, Kevin and Gary Hack. *Site Planning.* 3rd ed. Cambridge, Mass.: MIT Press. 1976.

Lynn, Frances M. "Public participation in risk management decisions: the right to know and right to act." Risk: Issues in Health and Safety, Vol.1 No.2, pp.95-102. 1990.

M.M. Dillion and Lapointe Consulting. *Town of Newmarket Residential Intensification Study.* 1991.

Macaulay Shiomi Howson in association with Jerome Markson Architects and Stephen Chait Consultants. *City of North York Residential Intensification: Arterial Roads and Existing Apartment Sites Phase II: Intensification Strategy,* 1991

Malone Given Parson Ltd. *Future Living Area Requirements.* 1993.

Marsh, P. *The Refurbishment of Commercial & Industrial Buildings.* London: Construction Press. 1983.

Marshall Macklin Monaghan. *Achieving Infrastructure Cost Efficiently/Effectively Through Alternative Planning Approaches,* 1992.

Marshall Macklin Monaghan. *Cornell: Municipal Infrastructure Cost Analysis.* 1994.

McDonald, Sue and Ann Borooah. *Achieving Housing and Environmental Objectives Through Residential Intensification: A Potential Partnership,* 1992.

McEachern, Wayne L. "Transit Friendly Land Use Planning: A Key Ingredient Supporting Environmental Quality and Economic Development," *Plan Canada,* 31:5, September 1991.

McLaren, Virginia. *Sustainable Development in Canada: From Concept to Practice: Vol I, II & III,* ICURR Press, Toronto, 1993.

Metropolitan Toronto, Municipality of. Community Services Department. Policy and Planning Division. *Housing Intensification Resource Kit.* 1993.

Metropolitan Toronto, Municipality of. Planning Department. *Retail Floor Space and Employment Characteristics in the Greater Toronto Area.* 1992b.

Metropolitan Toronto, Municipality of. Planning Department. *The Official Plan of Metropolitan Toronto: The Liveable Metropolis* . December 1994.

Municipal Affairs and Housing, Ministry of. *Comprehensive Set of Policy Statements: Implementation Guidelines.* 1994.

Municipal Affairs, Ministry of, and Ministry of Housing (MMA&H). *Apartments in Houses: Some Facts and Figures.* 1992.

Newman, Oscar. *Community of Interest.* New York: The MacMillan Company. 1980.

Newman, Oscar. *Defensible Space.* New York: The MacMillan Company. 1972.

Newman, P. and J. Kenworthy. "Gasoline Consumption and Cities: A Comparison of U.S. Cities with a Global Survey," *Journal of American Planning Association.* pp.24-37. Winter 1989.

Newman, P. and J. Kenworthy (1989), *Cities and Automobile Dependence: And international Sourcebook,* Gower, Aldershot.

O'Brien, Allan. *Municipal Consolidation in Canada and its Alternatives.* 1993.

Ouellet, Paule. *Environmental Policy Review of 15 Canadian Municipalities.* 2 Volumes. 1993.

Paehlke, Robert. *The Environmental Effects of Urban Intensification,* a report for the Municipal Planning Policy Branch, Ministry of Municipal Affairs, March, 1991.

Papanek, Victor. *Design for Human Scale,* (ed. K. Manasian & J. Towndrow), Van Nostrand Reinhold Company Inc., 1983.

Pearce, D. and K. Turner. *Economics of Natural Resources and the Environment.* Baltimore: John Hopkins University Press. 1991.

Peterborough, City of: Planning Division. *Downtown Residential Intensification Study.* 1991.

Petito Boyce, C. and T.C. Michelson. "Clean-up Standards for Petroleum Hydrocarbons. Part 2. Case Study Comparisons of site-specific cleanup standards with generic TPH standards." *Journal of Soil Contamination,* Vol.2, no.3, pp.265-280. 1993.

Pierce, David (ed.). Blueprint 2: *Greening the World Economy.* London: Earthscan Publications Ltd. 1991.

Pollution Probe. *The Costs of the Car: A Preliminary Study of the Environmental and Social Costs Associated with Private Car Use in Ontario*. 1991.

Porteous, Douglas J. *Environment & Behaviour: planning and everyday urban life*. Reading Mass.: Addison-Wesley Publishing Company, Inc., 1977.

Poyner, Barry. *Design Against Crime*. Cambridge: Cambridge University Press. 1983.

Real Estate Research Corporation. *The Costs of Sprawl*. 1974.

Rees, William E. & Roseland, Ross (1991), "Sustainable Communities: Planning for the 21st Century", *Plan Canada* 31:3 May, pp.15-24

Regional Municipality of Ottawa-Carleton. Planning Department. *Alternative Development Standards Proposals to Reduce Housing Costs*. 1992a.

Regional Municipality of Ottawa-Carleton. Planning Department. *Charette: Great Ideas for Small Spaces!* 1992b.

Regional Municipality of Ottawa-Carleton. Planning Department. *Small House Design Study: House Design Concepts based on Alternative Urban Development Standards*. 1992.

Renn, O. "Risk Communication: Towards a rational discourse with the Public." *Journal of Hazardous Materials*, Vol.29, no.3, pp.465-519. 1992.

Roseland, Mark. *Towards Sustainable Development*. Ottawa: National Round Table on the Environment and Economy. 1992.

Rusk, David. *Cities Without Suburbs*. Washington, D.C.: The Woodrow Wilson Center Press. 1993.

Rybczynski, Witold. "Living Smaller." *The Atlantic Monthly*. pp.64-79. February 1991.

Rydin, Yvonne. "Environmental Dimensions of Residential Development and the implications for Local Planning Practices", *Journal of Environmental Planning and Management,* Vol. 35 No.1, 1992.

Schrader-Frechette, K. "Scientific method, anti-foundationalism, and public decision-making." *Risk: Issues in Health and Safety*, Vol.1, no.1, pp.23-41. 1990.

Sheppard, S.C., P.M. Cureton, C. Gaudet, M.I. Sheppard. "The Development of assessment and remediation guidelines for contaminated soils, a review of the science." *Canadian Journal of Soil Science,* vol. 72, pp.359-394. 1992.

Shopsin, William. Restoring Old Buildings for Contemporary Uses. New York: Watson, Guptill. 1986.

Slack, Enid. *The Land Use Implications of Alternative Financial Tools: A Discussion Paper*. 1993.

Starr Group and Richard Drdla Associates. *Richmond Hill Municipal Housing Statement: Residential Intensification: Developing a Strategy for Richmond Hill*. 1990.

Starr Group. *Town of Ajax: Municipal Housing Statement, Residential Intensification Background Report*. 1992a.

Starr Group. *Town of Dundas: Municipal Housing Statement, Residential Intensification Background Report. Final Report*. 1992b.

Starr Group. *Town of Georgina Residential Intensification Background*. 1992c.

Starr Group. *Township of Cumberland: Municipal Housing Statement, Residential Intensification Final Report*. 1993.

Stone, Katherine E. and Dennis Martinek. "The Economic Consequences of Unmanaged Growth", *Western City*. November 1991.

Stren, R. and R. White. *African Cities in Crisis*. Boulder: Westview Press. 1989.

Sutherland, Scott, "Appropriate Responses to the Changing Needs of the Family". *Housing Young Families Affordably: Symposium Proceedings*. CMHC. 1990.

Thompson, Wilber. "The City as a Distorted Price System." *Psychology Today*. pp.28-33. 1968.

Tomalty, Ray. *The Compact Metropolis: Growth Management and Intensification in Vancouver, Toronto and Montreal*, ICURR (Intergovernmental Committee on Urban and Regional Research) 1996.

Toronto, City of, Planning & Development Department, Housing Department, Department of Public Works, *Housing on Toronto's Main Streets, Proposals Report*. 1989

Toronto, City of: Department of Public Works. *Water Conservation Report*. 1990.

Toronto, City of: Environmental Protection Office, Department of Public Health. *Identification of Potential Environmental Health Concerns of Soil Remediation Technologies*. 1991.

Toronto, City of: Planning and Development Department. *Housing on Toronto's Main Streets: A Design Competition*. 1990.

Transportation, Ministry of, and the Ministry of Municipal Affairs. *Transit-Supportive Land Use Planning Guidelines*. 1992.

Vojnovic, Igor. *Pathways Towards Sustainable Development and Sustainable Urban Forms*. Research Paper # 188, Centre for Urban & Community Studies, 1994.

Walker Wright Young Associates in association with Clayton Research Associates and Weir & Folds Barristers and Solicitors. *Housing Intensification Study for the City of Brampton*. 1991.

Walker Wright Young Associates. *Part A: Municipal Housing Statement for the City of Vaughan*. 1991a.

Walker Wright Young Associates. *Part B: Residential Intensification Analysis for the City of Vaughan*. 1991b.

Walker Wright Young Associates. *Part C: Housing Strategy for the City of Vaughan*. 1991c.

Walker Wright Young Associates. *Residential Intensification Study for the City of Mississauga*. 1992.

Walker, B. "Perspectives on qualitative risk assessment." *Journal of Environmental Health*, vol.55, no.1, pp.15-19. 1992

Warner North, D., F. Mirer, G.S. Omenn, P.J. Lioy, W. Cooper, S. Auerbach, M.A. Harwell, J.D. Graham, N. Kim, A.M. Finker and T.A. Burke. "Forum Two: Do we know enough to take a risk-based approach?" *EPA Journal*, vol.17, no.2, pp.31-39. 1991.

Wekerle, Gerda R. and Carolyn Whitzman. for the City of Toronto Planning Department. *A Working Guide for Planning And Designing Safer Urban Environments*. 1992.

Wekerle, Gerda R. and Carolyn Whitzman. *Safe Cities*. New York: Van Nostrand Reinhold. 1994.

Whyte, William H., *The Social Life of Small Urban Spaces*, The Conservation Foundation, Washington, D.C. 1980

Wong, J.J., R.A. Becker, E.G. Butler, G.M. Schum. "Looking Past Cleanup Numbers." In *Hydrocarbon contaminated soils and groundwater: Analysis Fate, Environment and public health effects*, P.T. Kostecki and E.J. Calabrese (eds.), Lewis Publishers, Boca Raton, Florida. 1991.

World Bank. *World Development Report: 1992*. Oxford: Oxford University Press. 1992.

World Commission on the Environment and Development. *Our Common Future*. Oxford: Oxford University Press. 1987.

York, City of: Planning Department. *Housing Strategy Study Official Plan Amendment*. 1992a.

York, City of: Planning Department. *Housing Strategy Study Questions & Answers and Draft Official Plan Amendment*. 1992b.